MY FIRST
ENCYCLOPEDIA

Melissa Blackwell Burke
Peg Hall

Consultant: Dana McMillan

Publications International, Ltd.

Melissa Blackwell Burke is a freelance writer of a variety of educational materials for both student and teacher use. A former elementary school teacher, she also writes children's literature and has published both fiction and nonfiction books.

Peg Hall has written numerous teacher guides and student activity books as well as fiction and nonfiction books for children. Her career has included experience as a classroom and reading resource teacher, an editor, and an education consultant. She currently works as a freelance writer from her home in coastal Massachusetts.

Consultant **Dana McMillan** is Director of Early Childhood Programs for The Learning Exchange. She has published more than 30 educational resource books, which have been sold both nationally and internationally, and she has developed many early childhood curricula, including an award-winning program for Binney & Smith (the makers of Crayola products).

Front cover: Rob Matheson/© Corbis (top left)

Devin Beebe/Index Stock Imagery, Inc.; © Corbis: Tiziana & Gianni Baldizzone; David Ball; Paul Barton; Niall Benvie; Bettmann; Georgina Bowater; Ralph A. Clevenger; Lloyd Cluff; Jerry Cooke; Jim Craigmyle; Darama; Bernard & Catherine Desjeux; Paul Edmondson; Firefly Production; Owen Franken; Gallo Images; Paul Gun; George Hall; Brownie Harris; Lindsay Hebberd; John Henley; Robert Holmes; Eric & David Hosking; Gavriel Jecan; Patrick Johns; Steve Kaufman; Lester Lefkowitz; Charles & Josette Lenars; Rob Lewine; Linda Lewis/Frank Lane Picture Agency; Craig Lovell; James Marshall; Rob Matheson; Joe McDonald; David Muench; Francesc Muntada; James Noble; Richard T. Nowitz; Charles O'Rear; Owaki-Kulla; Tim Pannell; Robert Pickett; Neil Rabinowitz; Steve Raymer; Reuters NewMedia; Jim Richardson; Joel W. Rogers; Georg Hans Roth; Galen Rowell; Kevin Schafer; Phil Schermeister; Ariel Skelley; Richard Hamilton Smith; Joseph Sohm; Paul A. Souders; Joel Stettenheim; James A. Sugar; Keren Su; Chase Swift/Vanuga Images; Karl Switak/Gallo Images; Craig Tuttle; Penny Tweedie; Kennan Ward; Tony Wilson-Bligh; Peter M. Wilson; Michael S. Yamashita; Jim Zuckerman; **Dale Glasgow; ImageState, Inc.:** International Stock; Bob Schatz; **Karl Lehmann/Lost World Art; Liquid Plastic Solutions; ©MapQuest.com; SuperStock:** Jerry Amster; Tom Brakefield; Alan Briere; Martin M. Bruce; Alice Garrard; William Hamilton; George Hunter; Tom Lipton; Charles Marden Fitch; Murat Myranci; Philadelphia Museum of Art, Pennsylvania/Giraudon, Paris; Nasi Sakura; Brad Sheard; Stock Montage; Yoshio Tomii; Alvis Upitis; Steve Vidler; **©1990 Sea World, Inc.; Scala/Art Resource; U.S. Government Web Sites for Kids; Wright State University Archives.**

Illustrations: Valda Glennie; Patrick Gnan

Additional Illustrations: Thomas Cranmer; Drew-Brook-Cormack Associates; Amy Paluch Epton; Brian Franczak; Brad Gaber; Mike Gardner; Peg Gerrity; Dale Gustafson; Zbigniew Jastrzebski; Bruce Long; Bob Masheris; Luis Rey; Richard Stergulz; Paula Wendland; Don Wieland; Kurt Williams.

Additional Photography: Siede Preis Photography; Silver Lining Digital, Inc.; Deborah Van Kirk.

Acknowledgments:
Page 12: Pablo Picasso, *The Three Musicians* (1921) © 2003 Estate of Pablo Picasso/Artists Rights Society (ARS), New York.

Contents

How to Use This Book

Have you ever had questions about the world? Do you sometimes wonder how things work? Have you ever wanted to learn about other places? Then this is the book for you!

My First Encyclopedia is the perfect book to help you learn about all kinds of things. You can read about how weather is made and how machines work. You can find out what the continent of Africa is like and learn how a building is constructed.

The words near a picture tell you about the photo. That way you can learn about what you're seeing.

To use the book, all you have to do is look up a subject you're interested in. The topics are in alphabetical order (A, B, C, D, and so on). So if you want to learn more about colors, look in the C's. Or if you want to find out about fish, turn to the F's.

You'll notice some special features in this book. Read the things on this page to learn all about them!

Try This
This box gives you fun experiments you can try on your own. It will help you understand even more about the topic.

Words to Know
The Words to Know box helps you with the hard words. Some words might be confusing, but if you look here, it will tell you what they mean.

It's a Fact!
This box has fun facts about the topic. You'll learn some amazing things!

More to Explore
The More to Explore box tells you where you can learn more about a subject. It lists other topics that will help you find out even more cool things!

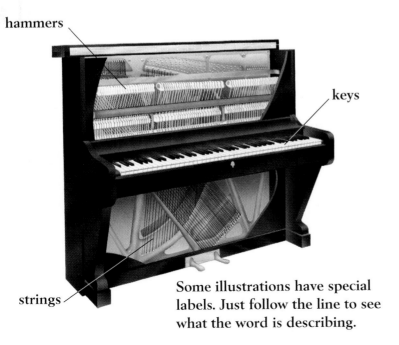

hammers

keys

strings

Some illustrations have special labels. Just follow the line to see what the word is describing.

Africa

Africa is the second-largest continent in the world. A continent is a large piece of land. Africa is the warmest of all the continents. It has areas of rain forest, grassland, and hot desert. This continent is home to an amazing variety of wildlife.

An African savanna

It's a Fact!

The name *Africa* probably came from a Latin word that means "sunny" or from a Greek word that means "without cold."

THE PEOPLE

Many different groups of people live in Africa. Hundreds of different languages are spoken there. One African language is called *Khoisan.* It is sometimes called "the click language" because many words are spoken by making clicking sounds with the tongue or throat.

In some parts of Africa, people live in modern cities. Other parts of Africa are still like they were thousands of years ago. Some people live in simple villages without running water or electricity. Some people are *nomads,* which means they don't live in one place. Instead, they live in tents and travel all over with their herds of animals.

In the southern part of Africa, people often wear clothes with bright colors. Colorful jewelry is also common.

WILDLIFE

Africa is known for its interesting wildlife. It has some of the most amazing animals in the whole world. For example, the African elephant is the biggest animal on land.

The cheetah is a beautiful spotted cat that lives in the wide open spaces of Africa. It is the fastest animal on land. A cheetah can easily run as fast as a car!

You have probably seen lots of giraffes at the zoo. In Africa, giraffes roam all around the grassland areas. Giraffes are the world's tallest animals.

African elephant

Giraffe

Cheetah

More to Explore

Clothing • Desert • Grasslands • Language

The baobab tree grows well in the dry lands of Africa. It can store water in its trunk, so it always has enough to drink.

Words to Know

desert: *an area of hot, dry land*

savanna: *an area of flat grassland with few trees*

nomads: *people who travel from place to place*

THE LAND

The land in Africa is very wild and beautiful. The continent has many interesting land features. One is the Great Rift Valley, which is the longest crack in the Earth's crust. The crack is thousands of miles long!

Africa also has the biggest desert in the world. The Sahara covers millions of miles.

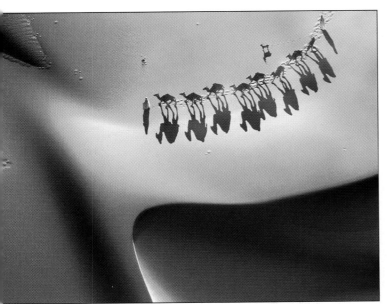

The Sahara

Aircraft

Aircraft are flying machines. There are lots of different types of aircraft, including airplanes, helicopters, hang gliders, and hot air balloons. Airplanes were invented about 100 years ago. Back then, very few people got to ride in aircraft. Today, millions of people fly on planes each day.

Spaceships, such as the space shuttle, take people into outer space. A very strong rocket sends the ship into space. Then pilots drive the shuttle around, a lot like a regular plane.

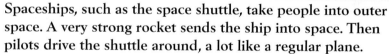

Helicopters can really move! They can fly forward, backward, sideways, up, down, or even stay in one spot. The blades on the top of the helicopter go around and around. They keep the craft up in the air. Helicopters are very useful. They are even used to help rescue people.

Hot air balloons have been around a long time. They were invented to help people travel, but they aren't very useful for that. They are now used mostly for fun. Hot flames heat air that fills the balloon. Since hot air rises, the balloon lifts off the ground. People ride in the basket to enjoy the trip.

Words to Know

invent: *to create for the first time*

pilot: *person in charge of flying an aircraft*

Otto Lilienthal and his glider

The Wright Flyer

THE HISTORY OF THE PLANE

People tried to fly for hundreds of years. Some people built wings and tried to fly like a bird. Other people made machines, but most of them didn't work. Then a man named Otto Lilienthal built a glider, which is a plane without an engine. His glider actually worked! Later, two Americans named Wilbur and Orville Wright made and flew an aircraft powered by an engine.

Over the years, planes have changed a lot. Old planes weren't very safe and were very small. New planes have gotten safer, and they can carry lots of people. Planes have also gotten much faster over the years.

It's a Fact!
• The first landing on the moon was only 66 years after the first airplane ride.
• The largest airliner today can carry up to 567 people.

More to Explore

Inventions • Space

Amphibians

Amphibians are cold-blooded. They are born in water and breathe with gills, just like fish. As amphibians grow, their gills become lungs. Adult amphibians live on land and in the water. Frogs, toads, salamanders, and newts are all amphibians.

THE LIFE OF A FROG

An adult frog lays eggs.

A tadpoles hatches from an egg.

The tadpole begins to grow legs.

The tadpole's tail disappears. It is ready to live on land.

The tadpole becomes a frog.

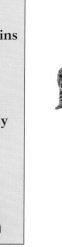

HOW CAN YOU TELL A FROG FROM A TOAD?

FROG
Smooth skin
Webbed feet
Long back legs
Lives in or near water

TOAD
Dry, bumpy skin
Not much webbing between toes
Shorter back legs
Spends most of the time on land

It's a Fact!
• Newts and salamanders are a lot alike. There aren't very many of them either. There are only 350 kinds in the world!
• Did you know that some frogs can fly? There are tree frogs in the rain forest that fly by spreading their webbed feet out and gliding through the air!

Words to Know

webbed: *skin stretched between fingers or toes*

More to Explore

Lakes and Ponds • Wetlands

Antarctica

Antarctica is one of the seven continents. This large piece of land is covered by a thick sheet of ice. Antarctica is the coldest place on Earth. Because of these bad conditions, few people are found there. Scientists and some tourists visit, but they don't make Antarctica their home.

Antarctica's ice has 70 percent of the world's freshwater.

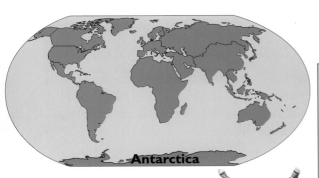

Antarctica

Words to Know

continent: *a large body of land*

Southern elephant seal

ANTARCTIC WILDLIFE

Penguins like the cold weather in Antarctica. They huddle in big groups to stay warm. The emperor penguin is the biggest kind of penguin.

Emperor penguin

Only a few tiny plants can grow in the extreme cold of Antarctica. Not many insects live there either. But there is still a lot of sea life! Many birds and seals, such as this southern elephant seal, live in the Antarctic.

Krill are very important to wildlife in Antarctica. These little sea animals are food for seals, whales, penguins, and more. Lots of animals wouldn't survive without krill to feed on.

Krill

Thousands of scientists work in Antarctica. They live and work at research stations. They study the ice, the weather, and the wildlife. There are about 30 research stations like this one in Antarctica.

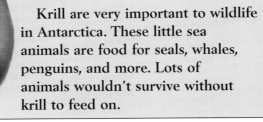

More to Explore

Ocean • Weather

11

Art

Art is what people create that has beauty or special meaning. There are many kinds of art. Drawings, photos, and even some baskets are all works of art. People who make art are called artists. Sometimes artists make art to show the world how they see a certain thing. Sometimes they just want to create something pretty. Artists make art for lots of reasons.

A work of art doesn't always have to look exactly like the thing it's supposed to show. Pablo Picasso, who created this, made art that looked a little different.

The Sistine Chapel in Italy has beautiful paintings on its ceiling. The paintings show scenes from the Bible. They are very famous pictures. People travel from far away just to see them.

Try This

Michelangelo is a famous artist who painted the ceiling of the Sistine Chapel. It took him more than four years to finish his artwork there. Get a feel for how Michelangelo had to work! Tape some paper underneath a table or desk. Lie under the table, and paint or draw a picture.

ALL KINDS OF ART

Drawing. Artists often use pencils to make quick drawings.

Graphic Design. Artists work on computers to create images.

Painting. Artists use brushes and paint to create art.

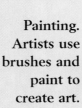

Photography. Artists use cameras to make a work of art.

Sculpture. Artists form or carve art in stone, wood, clay, or metal.

Weaving. Artists use fabric and other cloth to create art.

Every culture has different types of art. For example, in Mexico some people make clay pitchers that they paint with colorful designs. And in Japan some beautiful art is carved from a pretty green stone called *jade*.

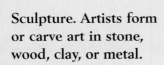

More to Explore

Colors • Religion

Asia

Asia is the world's largest continent. A continent is a huge piece of land. Asia has land with lots of different types of weather. Some of the land there is hot and dry. Other parts are cold and icy. Still other parts get lots of rain. Asia is bordered by three oceans— the Arctic Ocean, the Pacific Ocean, and the Indian Ocean. Asia includes many islands.

Hong Kong is a big city in Asia. More than 7 million people live there.

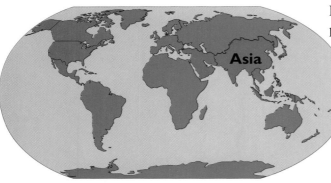

It's a Fact!

Asia includes the highest point on Earth, Mount Everest. It also includes the lowest point on Earth, the Dead Sea.

Words to Know

desert: *an area of hot, dry land*

endangered species: *a type of animal of which there are few left*

island: *land that is surrounded by water on all sides*

ocean: *a large body of water*

The giant rafflesia is only found in a few Asian rain forests. It is the biggest flower in the whole world. It can weigh almost 25 pounds!

Vietnam

Mount Everest

THE LAND

Asia has some very high mountains. Many of these are a group of mountains called the Himalayas (hi-muh-LAY-uhs). Mount Everest is the highest mountain in the world. It is in the Himalaya Mountains.

Asia also has many famous rivers. Some, like the Yangtze and the Yellow River, are among the world's longest rivers. Others are important because they were homes to some of the world's first people.

THE PEOPLE

More than half the people in the world live in Asia. They belong to many different groups, and they speak many different languages.

Asia has a very long and interesting history. Many of the world's oldest cultures began in Asia. All of the major religions (Buddhism, Christianity, Hinduism, Islam, Judaism, and Sikhism) were started there, too.

Asia has many of the world's biggest cities. Most people still live in the country in Asia, though. They work on farms and live in small towns and villages.

WILDLIFE

Because there are so many different types of land in Asia, the continent is home to an incredible collection of wildlife. Unfortunately, many of these animals are dying out. Animals that are in danger of disappearing like this are called *endangered species.*

There aren't many giant pandas left in Asia. The giant panda has beautiful black-and-white coloring and eats almost nothing but a woody type of grass called bamboo.

The orangutan is also endangered. Orangutans are big apes that like to move around by swinging through the trees. Their name means "man of the forest."

The Sumatran rhinoceros is in danger, too. It is the smallest of the rhinoceros family, but it still weighs almost 2,000 pounds!

Sumatran rhinoceros

Giant panda

Orangutan

More to Explore

Endangered Species • Farms • Grasslands • Mountains • Religion • Rivers and Streams

15

Australia

Australia is one of the world's seven continents. It is the only continent that is made up of only one country. Much of Australia is flat, hot, and dry land. Australia is located between two oceans, the Indian Ocean and the Pacific Ocean.

Sydney, Australia

THE PEOPLE

The native people of Australia are called Aborigines (a-buh-RIJ-nees). There are many different groups of Aborigines. They all have strong beliefs about staying in touch with the land and living things.

Today most people in Australia live in cities along the coast. People in Australia speak English, but they sort of have a language of their own, too. They use their own special words and phrases, such as "bicky" for cookie and "mate" for friend.

Many people in Australia work in farming or raising sheep. Mining, or taking minerals from the ground, is also important in Australia. Lots of coal and diamonds are found in Australia.

It's a Fact!
The seasons in Australia are opposite from the seasons in North America. So, when it's winter in North America, it's summer in Australia. If a child in North America is building a snowman, a child is Australia may be surfing or having a beach party.

Words to Know
coast: *land near the shore of a body of water*
continent: *a large body of land*
ocean: *a large body of water*

Try This
A traditional birthday treat in Australia is Hundreds and Thousands sandwiches. To make these, cut the crusts from white bread. Spread butter on the bread. Add "hundreds and thousands," which are rainbow-color sprinkles. Cut the sandwiches into triangles, and enjoy!

Australian Aborigines

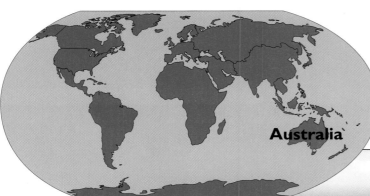

THE LAND

About one-third of Australia is desert, which is very hot and dry land. Much of the rest is plains, which are flat and have very few trees.

Australia also has the famous Great Barrier Reef. Tiny sea animals called *coral* created this structure in the ocean. The Great Barrier Reef is home to more than 400 different kinds of coral and about 1,500 different kinds of fish.

It's a Fact!

There are more sheep in Australia than people! For every one person, there are seven sheep.

The Great Barrier Reef

Duck-billed platypus

Koala

WILDLIFE

Australia has some unusual animals that don't live anywhere else in the world. The kangaroo is a famous Australian animal. It carries its young in a pouch on the front of its body. Kangaroos get around by jumping, so they have very powerful legs.

The koala also carries its young around in a pouch. It might look like a bear, but it's really not related to bears at all. In fact, it's related to the kangaroo!

The platypus is a very special animal. The platypus is a mammal, and most mammals (such as humans) give birth to live babies. But the platypus lays eggs for its babies!

More to Explore

Desert • Farms • Mammals • Ocean • The Seasons

Kangaroo

Bicycles

A bicycle, or bike, is a machine with two wheels. The parts of a bike work together to turn a rider's power into movement. Bikes help people move around quickly and easily under their own power. Millions of people around the world ride bicycles each day.

Words to Know

sprocket: a wheel with pointed teeth

More to Explore

Machines

The rider sits in the saddle.

The sprocket turns the chain, which moves the wheel.

The rider moves the bike by pushing the pedals.

The rider steers with the handlebar.

The rider stops the bike by using the brakes.

BICYCLES THEN AND NOW

Bicycles were first built about 200 years ago. Some of the first bikes had their pedals attached to the front wheel. Every time the pedal made a whole circle, the front wheel turned around once, too. That was a lot of pedaling!

Today's bicycles have pedals that are attached to a *sprocket*, which is a small metal wheel with teeth in it. The sprocket is connected to the back wheel by a chain. Turning the pedals turns the sprocket. When the sprocket turns, it pulls the chain. This makes the back wheel turn. As the back wheel turns, it moves the bike forward.

Birds

Birds are the only kind of animals that have feathers. They have two scaly feet and two wings. Most birds use their wings to fly. To have babies, birds lay eggs with tough shells. The parents then keep the eggs warm until the baby birds are born, or hatch.

Most birds have special parts of their body that help them fly. For example, many birds have long, straight feathers that help them stay up in the air. Some birds cannot fly at all, though. The ostrich is a bird that doesn't fly. It is the biggest bird in the world, but it has tiny wings. Instead of flying, the ostrich runs very fast on its long, strong legs.

Birds are some of the most beautiful animals because they come in so many bright colors.

BIRD NESTS

Most birds build nests where they lay eggs and raise their young. Nests can be made from lots of things, including sticks, grass, and mud. Some birds even like to find pieces of string and little bits of hair to help build their nests.

Birds build nests in all kinds of places! Nests can be in tree branches, on rooftops, in caves, or even on the ground. If you see a nest, watch it from far away. Don't get too close, or you might scare the bird and the babies!

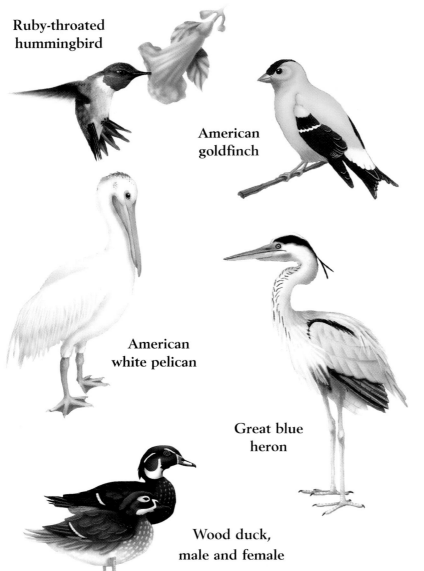

Ruby-throated hummingbird

American goldfinch

American white pelican

Great blue heron

Wood duck, male and female

BEAKS AND FEET

You can tell a lot about a bird just from its bill and its feet. A bird's bill, or *beak*, is its nose and mouth. A bird has just the right kind of beak to help it get the food it needs.

For example, a goldfinch eats lots of seeds. It has a short, strong bill that is good for cracking the seeds open.

A long, sharp bill is good for spearing fish. The heron spends a lot of time using its beak to fish for food in the water.

A bird also has feet that match the way it lives. Bird feet come in many different shapes.

Birds that spend a lot of time swimming in the water have webbed feet. Webbed feet have skin stretched between the toes. A pelican has webbed feet.

Some birds that like to walk in water have feet with toes that are far apart. The wide-spaced toes help them keep their balance and keep them from sinking in the mud. Herons have wide-spaced toes.

It's a Fact!
One reason birds can fly is that they have strong bones that are very light. Some of the bones are even hollow.

Some birds fly thousands of miles every year. When the weather becomes colder, the birds fly south to warmer places. They return to the north when the weather becomes warm again. This is called *migration* (my-GRAY-shun).

The Body

Your body is a living thing. Like everything that is alive, it is made up of millions of tiny parts called cells. Different kinds of cells make up different parts of the body, such as bones, muscles, and skin. These parts all work together to help you breathe, walk, and do everything else.

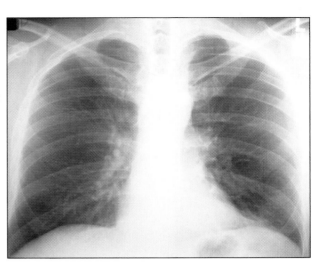

X rays are special photos that help doctors see the bones inside a person's body.

BONES AND SKELETON

Your body has 206 different bones. These bones fit together to make up your skeleton. Without your skeleton, you wouldn't be able to walk, stand, or even sit up. Some bones are long, such as the bones in your arms and legs. Others are tiny, such as some of the bones inside your ears.

It's a Fact!
• When you were born, you had more bones than you do now! Babies are born with more than 300 bones. Some very small bones join together as the baby grows.
• Your hands have 26 bones each.
• The inside of a bone is not hard like the outside. The inside is a little bit spongy.

THE NERVOUS SYSTEM

Nerves are like tiny wires that run through your body. They carry messages back and forth along a spinal cord that runs from your hips to your brain. Together, the nerves, brain, and spinal cord are called the *nervous system.*

When your foot touches something hot, the nerves in your skin send a message. The message flashes along the nerves in your foot and leg to the spinal cord and then to your brain. Your brain sends a message to your muscles to pull your foot away from the heat. All this happens in less than a second!

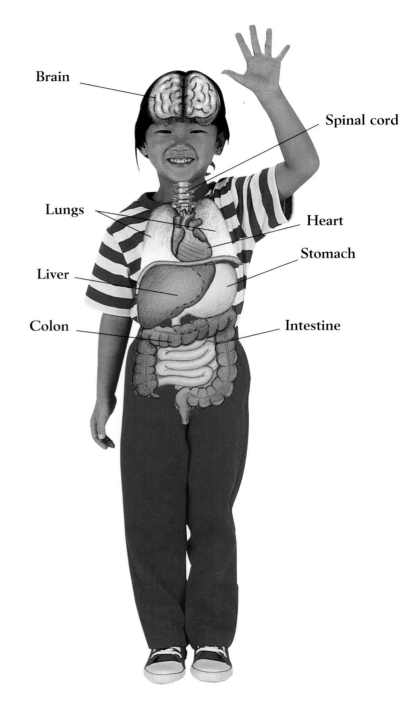

Brain

Spinal cord

Lungs

Heart

Stomach

Liver

Colon

Intestine

Words to Know

cell: *the smallest part of any living thing*
energy: *the ability to move and work*
nutrients: *parts of food the body uses to grow and stay healthy*

Try This

Your ribs are the bones in your chest. Press your hands gently against your ribs. Can you feel how they form a kind of cage? If you get bumped or hit in the chest, this cage will help protect your heart and lungs.

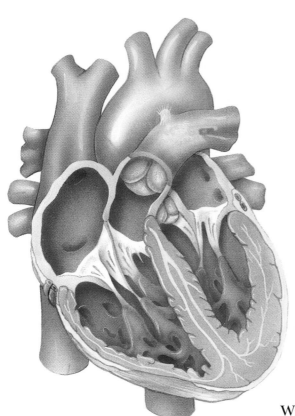

HEART

Your heart is a very strong muscle that never stops working. It pumps blood through tubes called *blood vessels.* The blood carries nutrients and oxygen to every part of your body. Then the blood travels back to the heart. It picks up more nutrients and oxygen there and carries them around the body. This happens over and over!

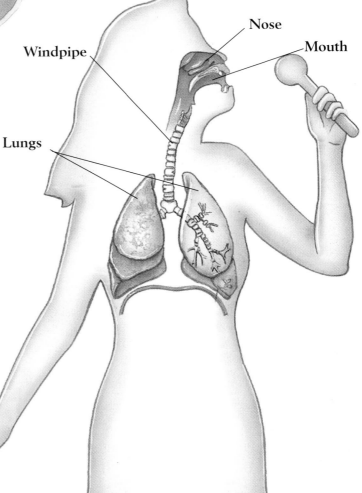

Nose

Mouth

Windpipe

Lungs

LUNGS

The air around you is filled with the oxygen that your body needs to stay alive. But how does the oxygen get inside your body? Your lungs work hard to do this job.

When you breathe, you take in oxygen through your mouth and nose. The oxygen travels through a tube called the *windpipe* until it reaches the lungs. Inside the lungs, the oxygen goes into your blood. The blood then carries it all through your body.

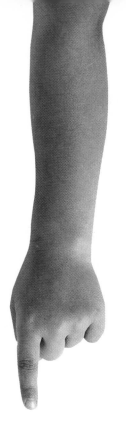

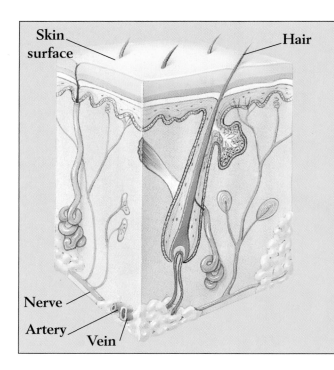

Skin surface

Hair

Nerve

Artery

Vein

SKIN

Your body is covered with a thin layer of skin. Skin is stretchy and waterproof. It is also alive. New skin cells grow every day. Old skin cells dry up and fall off every day.

Skin is important because it protects your body from heat and cold. It also keeps germs from getting inside. Your skin is full of special nerve endings that give you your sense of touch. These nerve endings tell you when something is hot, cold, sharp, and so on.

MUSCLES

Muscles let your body move. You use tiny muscles to blink or smile. You use large muscles to walk, run, or throw a ball.

Muscles move in two ways. They can *contract,* or get tighter. They can also *relax,* or get looser. When you want to pick up a ball, your brain sends a message to your hand muscles. It tells them to contract and grab the ball. When you let the ball go, your brain sends a message to your muscles telling them to relax.

Some muscles do their work even if you never think about them. These are called *involuntary muscles.* Your heart is an involuntary muscle. You don't have to make it beat; it just does its job.

It's a Fact!

The human body starts out as one cell. That cell divides and grows. By the time a baby is born, its body has millions and millions of cells.

More to Explore

Food • Health • Life Cycle • The Senses

Books

Books are pages of paper that are fastened together. There are two main types of books: fiction and nonfiction. Fiction books are made-up stories. Nonfiction books are based on facts. Both types of books are very important. Books help to teach and entertain people.

HOW BOOKS USED TO BE MADE

Long ago, people didn't have a system for writing. They could only tell stories or share news by talking. Then people began to write things down. Books were written by hand. It took a long time, and books cost a lot of money.

Then the printing press was invented. This machine allowed many copies of a book to be made. When printing became cheaper, books were available for more people. Today, computers have made printing books cheaper and easier than ever.

It's a Fact!
The first books were printed in China. People carved characters onto wooden blocks and used them for printing.

The paper in books is usually made from wood. The wood is first ground up in a factory. Then it is mixed with water and chemicals. This mixture is put into a machine that stretches and presses it into one big sheet. After it dries, the paper is polished. That helps make it smooth.

More to Explore

Computers • Inventions • Mass Media • Trees

Buildings

A building is a structure put together by people. Every building has a purpose. It may be a place for people to live (such as a home), work (such as an office), shop (such as a store), or just have fun (such as a movie theater). People have created buildings since very early times. Buildings look a lot different now than they did back then!

Egyptians built the pyramids a long time ago. They buried their leaders inside them when they died. The buildings are huge and made of stone.

The Taj Mahal (tahzh muh-HALL) in India was built by an emperor long ago. He built it for his wife, who had died. He wanted to show how much he loved her.

Skyscrapers are very tall buildings that are usually made out of stone or metal. Some skyscrapers, such as the Empire State Building in New York City, are famous. Lots of tourists visit them.

A person who helps design, or plan, a building is called an *architect* (AHR-ki-tekt).

More to Explore

Construction • Homes • Jobs

Cars

Automobiles have been around for about 100 years. In that time, they have gone through many changes. Today, millions of people around the world drive cars. These machines on the move carry people and goods from one place to another.

More to Explore

Inventions • Machines • Metal

When more and more people drive cars, the roads get very crowded! Automobiles also cause pollution. If too many people drive cars, it's not good for the air.

Most cars have a place for at least one passenger.

The hood covers the car's inside parts.

The trunk is a place for things you need to carry.

The engine sits under the hood. It powers the car.

The driver steers the car along the road.

The tires allow the car to move.

The body of most cars is built of metal.

CARS PAST AND PRESENT

Cars have changed the way people live. People used to travel in different ways, such as by horse or by train. Cars have made it easy to get to places quickly.

Automobiles weren't always fast, though. The first cars were very slow and not very safe.

Cars didn't even have roofs back then! It took a long time to build one car, and it cost a lot of money to make.

Today, cars are made of strong metal. They can move quickly. Millions of new cars are built each year.

Castles

Long ago, castles were built as safe places to live. People from the outside couldn't get in easily, so the people on the inside were protected. A castle was usually the home of an important person, such as a king or warrior lord. Many other people also lived behind the castle walls. The castle and its land were almost like a little town.

Many castles are still standing in Europe. Thousands of people visit castles each year to learn about the buildings.

THE MAKINGS OF A CASTLE

Towers were places to watch for an attack or to defend the castle.

Narrow openings allowed defenders to shoot arrows at attackers.

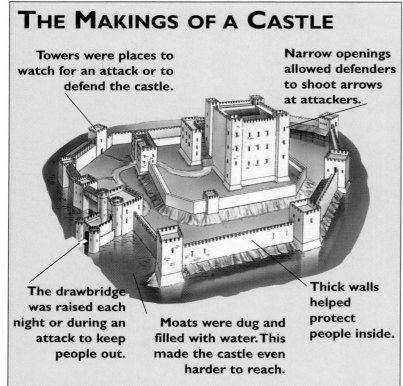

The drawbridge was raised each night or during an attack to keep people out.

Moats were dug and filled with water. This made the castle even harder to reach.

Thick walls helped protect people inside.

Castle life was built around a courtyard. There were rooms for people to sleep in, a kitchen, horse stables, a chapel, a drinking well, and storage areas. There was also a large apartment for the castle owner. Feasts, weddings, and other celebrations were held in a big room called the *great hall*.

Castles in Japan look different, but they were still built to protect people.

It's a Fact!
People who lived in the castle hid in the dungeon if enemies got inside the building.

More to Explore

Asia • Buildings • Europe • Homes

28

Clothing

Clothing is all the things that people wear—shirts, pants, dresses, shoes, hats, and more. There are lots of reasons people dress the way they do. People sometimes dress for the weather. For example, if people live somewhere hot then they might wear light clothing.

You probably have lots of different types of clothes. For example, you might have clothes for school and different clothes for play. And maybe you have special clothes for when you need to dress up.

People wear special clothes to do some jobs. These are called *uniforms.* The clothes might protect the person or make a job easier to do, such as with firefighters. Firefighter uniforms protect them from smoke, heat, and flames.

There are lots of different groups of people in Kenya. The national dress of these groups usually has a lot of bright colors and beaded jewelry.

Traditional clothes of a country are called its *national dress*. In many places, people only wear the special clothing on holidays or other occasions. The kimono is the national dress of Japan. It is worn by both men and women.

In the desert of Saudi Arabia, a head cloth called a *kaffiyeh* helps keep the sun and sand out of people's faces.

More to Explore

Holidays • Jobs • Rescue • Weather

Colors

Your world is filled with colors—the blue sky, a red apple, a bright yellow bird, and so much more. All the colors you see depend on light. When light goes in your eyes, a special part of the eye works to see color.

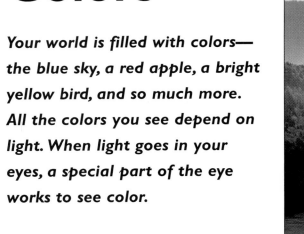

A rainbow is when water drops in the air act like prisms. They separate the colors in sunlight. The color of the bands in a rainbow are in the same order as they are in a prism.

LIGHT WAVES

Light is a kind of energy. It travels through the air in invisible waves called *light waves.* Light waves go up and down, much like the waves in the ocean.

Colors are part of light. Each color makes it own kind of light wave. Sunlight has the same amount of all the colors. Because of that, none of the colors show up. Sunlight is called *white light.* It is light that seems to have no color.

A kind of lens called a *prism* can show you the colors in sunlight. Light bends when it shines through a prism. As the light bends, each color goes in a different direction. The colors are separated, and you can see each one by itself. The colors are always in the same order.

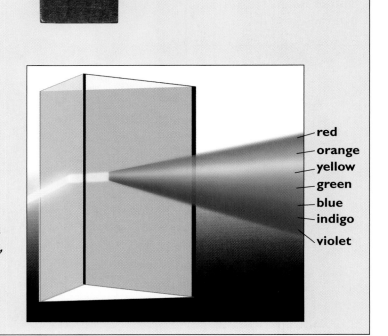

red
orange
yellow
green
blue
indigo
violet

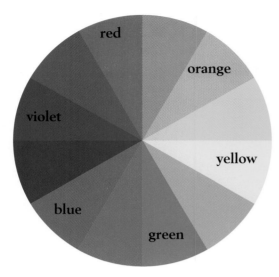

Red, blue, and yellow are called *primary colors.* A primary color cannot be made by mixing other colors. Orange, green, and purple are called *secondary colors.* Secondary colors are made by mixing two primary colors.

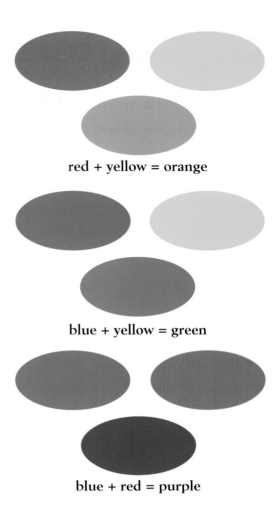

red + yellow = orange

blue + yellow = green

blue + red = purple

WHY COLOR IS IMPORTANT

Colors aren't just pretty. They also do an important job. Colors really help plants and animals. For example, color is what attracts bees to flowers. The bees then spread pollen to flowers and help them grow. Humans also use color to signal or communicate with one another. A red stoplight tells drivers to stop. Also, colored uniforms tell us which team is which in sports.

It's a Fact!

A special part of the eye called *cones* lets you see color. Cones are at the back of the eyeball.

More to Explore

Light • The Senses

Computers

A computer is a machine that processes information. This information is called data. Computers can also store data. A computer can do difficult tasks. One part of the computer works like an electronic brain. It breaks down the task into small parts. It solves simple problems one at a time. It works very quickly. People use computers to do work and to communicate.

More to Explore

Electricity • Inventions • Machines

Computers have been around for about 60 years. The first computers were huge. Some were the size of a whole room! They used a lot of electricity.

PARTS OF A COMPUTER

These computer parts allow the user to put data in and get data out.

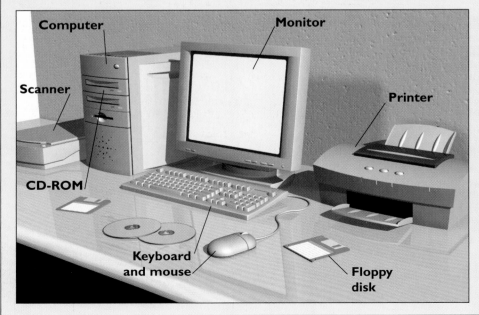

Computer • Monitor • Scanner • Printer • CD-ROM • Keyboard and mouse • Floppy disk

• The screen, which is called a *monitor,* shows words and pictures.
• The keyboard and mouse allow the user to type words and to make choices.
• The computer performs tasks and stores data.
• Floppy disks can hold information from a computer.
• CD-ROMs are another way to store data.
• A scanner can read pictures and photographs. It then turns them into data.
• The printer takes words and pictures from the monitor and prints them on paper.

Construction

The word construct *means "to build."* **Construction** *is the act of building something. Since early times, people have built all kinds of things. People are still busy building. They build homes and other structures. They build roads to link one place to another. People build bridges to cross waterways. They build tunnels to pass through mountains or other things.*

HOW A ROAD IS BUILT

It takes a few different steps to build a road:

1. The ground is leveled. Trenches are dug.

2. Drains are laid. These will carry water away from the road.

3. Layers of stone and soil are put down.

4. Asphalt, a special material for roads, is laid.

5. Stripes are painted on the road.

HOW A SKYSCRAPER IS BUILT

People build tall buildings in order to take up less ground space. A skyscraper starts with a pit dug into the ground. A strong concrete foundation is then poured.

The inner frame of the building is put up next. It is usually made of steel or concrete. The floors and walls are then added. The walls are often glass. The inside of the building is then completed.

Try This

Create your own tall building! Gather empty boxes of different sizes. Try stacking the boxes in different ways to see which setup makes the tallest and sturdiest building. Hint: Look at pictures of several tall buildings. Notice the wide, strong bases!

The Golden Gate Bridge

MACHINES THAT BUILD

Big, heavy machines do a lot of work on construction sites.

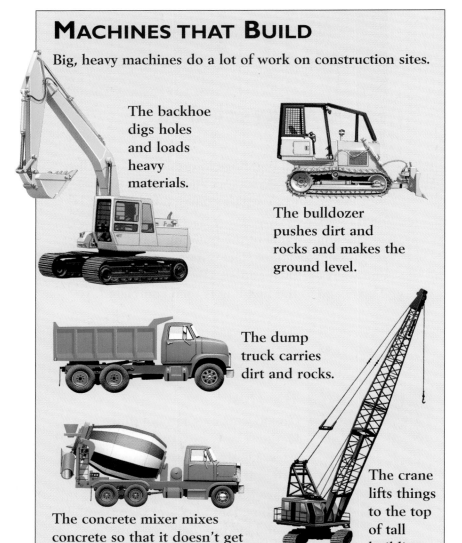

The backhoe digs holes and loads heavy materials.

The bulldozer pushes dirt and rocks and makes the ground level.

The dump truck carries dirt and rocks.

The crane lifts things to the top of tall buildings.

The concrete mixer mixes concrete so that it doesn't get hard until it is poured.

CROSSING BRIDGES

Long ago, people built simple bridges. They laid a tree trunk across a river, or they made a path of stones in shallow water. Today, people build many kinds of bridges. They use concrete and steel.

TUNNELING THROUGH

Tunnels help people travel more easily and quickly. Tunnels can be dug right through a mountain. They can also be dug underneath a river or busy roadway.

More to Explore

Buildings • Jobs • Machines

Dance

Dance is the movement of the body to music. People have been dancing since very early times. In many countries, people have traditional dances as part of special celebrations. For these dances, people often wear costumes.

Words to Know

costume: *special clothes that set a tone*

prop: *an item or a piece of equipment used in theater or dance*

WHY PEOPLE DANCE

People dance for a lot of reasons. Some people dance so they can tell stories with their bodies. Some people dance for exercise. Some people dance just for fun.

Other times people dance as part of their culture. Folk dances are traditional dances for a group of people. These dances are sometimes part of celebrations or worship.

Some dancers wear special clothes called *costumes* to perform their dances. Sometimes they use *props*. These props might be musical instruments, such as bells or sticks, or a sword or a shield used to act out a story.

Try This

Stand tall and straight. Turn your feet out so your heels are touching and your toes are pointed away from each other. Get your feet to make as straight a line as possible. In ballet, this move is called *first position*.

Ballet is a graceful style of dance. It combines dance, music, and acting. A ballet tells a story.

Some dances, such as tap dancing, you do alone. Other types of dancing you do with a partner. The partners work together to perform the dance.

Traditional dance in the country of Bali (BAH-lee) is important. The dance usually tells a story and often includes masks.

It's a Fact!

• Some dancers have to wear special shoes. Tap dancers wear shoes with metal discs on the bottom. These discs make tapping sounds on the ground during the dance.

• The belly dance is one of the world's oldest dances. It has been around for thousands of years.

More to Explore

Clothing • Holidays • Music • Religion

Democracy

A democracy is a kind of government. It is run by everyday people—not just people who were born to be kings or leaders. Every person who lives in a democracy can't be a leader, though. They all get to elect, or choose, their leaders. In a democracy, people have choices and freedom. The United States government is a democracy.

The first people signed the Declaration of Independence on July 4 in 1776. Today, Independence Day is on July 4 in the United States.

HOW VOTING WORKS

A person says she or he would like to be a leader. People make a choice and vote on who they think should be the leader. The votes are counted. → The person who gets the most votes wins.

THE UNITED STATES AND DEMOCRACY

More than two hundred years ago, the United States was part of England. Americans decided they wanted to rule themselves. A group of American leaders wrote the Declaration of Independence. This paper explained to the King of England that America wanted to be its own country.

Americans fought a war to be free. General George Washington led the fight against the English. People elected him the first President, or leader, of the United States.

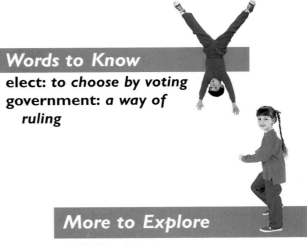

Words to Know
elect: *to choose by voting*
government: *a way of ruling*

More to Explore
U.S. Presidents

Desert

A desert is a place that is dry all the time. Deserts get less than ten inches of rain in a whole year. The land in a desert can be sandy or rocky.

Words to Know

nocturnal: *active at night*

It's a Fact!

Many desert animals are nocturnal. They sleep during the hot daytime and come out to eat at night when it is cool.

An underground stream or spring can make a pool of water in the desert. Plants and trees grow there. This area is called an *oasis.*

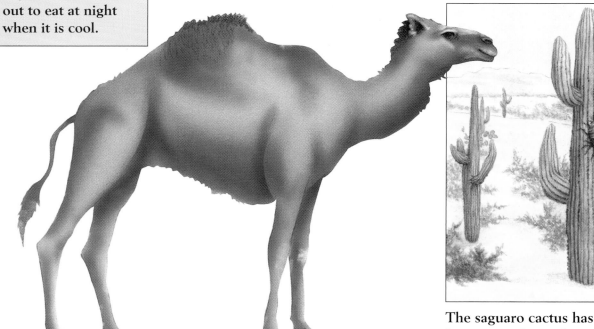

The camel is perfectly suited to living in the desert! It has wide, flat feet that make it easy to walk on sand. The camel stores fat in its hump. If things get too dry, it can use that fat as food and water.

The saguaro cactus has many ways to keep every drop of water it can get. The cactus has a waxy covering that keeps water from escaping into the air. When it rains, the cactus swells up with stored water. It doesn't want to miss out on any of the water!

Desert animals and plants have special ways to survive. The fennec fox has huge ears that let heat escape from its body.

More to Explore

Africa • Asia • Australia • North America • Plants • Trees • Weather

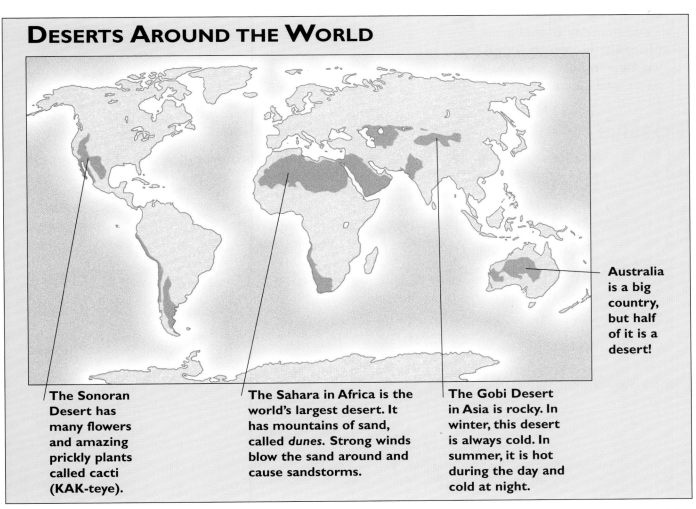

DESERTS AROUND THE WORLD

Australia is a big country, but half of it is a desert!

The Sonoran Desert has many flowers and amazing prickly plants called cacti (KAK-teye).

The Sahara in Africa is the world's largest desert. It has mountains of sand, called *dunes*. Strong winds blow the sand around and cause sandstorms.

The Gobi Desert in Asia is rocky. In winter, this desert is always cold. In summer, it is hot during the day and cold at night.

Dinosaurs

Dinosaurs are animals that lived millions of years ago, long before there were any humans. Some dinosaurs were the largest animals that have ever lived on Earth. Scientists learn about dinosaurs by studying bones and other signs these creatures left behind.

Scientists can sometimes put all the pieces of a dinosaur skeleton together. These skeletons are usually shown in museums.

Words to Know
jungle: *hot, wet forest where many plants grow*
minerals: *materials found in water and the Earth, such as salt and calcium*

FOSSILS
A fossil is what is left of something that lived long ago. Most dinosaurs did not become fossils. But some did. Here is how a fossil might have been made:

1. A dinosaur died. Most of its body rotted away, leaving just the bones.

2. The bones were covered with layers of mud and sand.

3. More layers of mud and sand were added over millions of years. The layers pressed so hard together they became rock. The bones turned into rock, too.

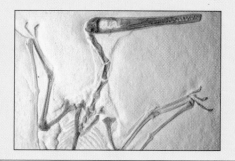

4. Earthquakes broke the rock apart. The bones that had been in the rock moved, too.

5. Wind and rain wore away the rock. At last, some fossils showed through. Scientists could then dig them out and study them.

THE TIME OF DINOSAURS

There were many dinosaurs, but they didn't all live at the same time. Different times had different dinosaurs. Then the dinosaurs suddenly died out. No one is quite sure why they became extinct. It is a science mystery!

248 million years ago

TRIASSIC PERIOD

The first dinosaurs live.

Euskelosaurus

Barapasaurus

213 million years ago

JURASSIC PERIOD

Dilophosaurus

Compsognathus

144 million years ago

CRETACEOUS PERIOD

Tyrannosaurus

Triceratops

65 million years ago

Dinosaurs die out.

4 million years ago

The first humans live.

WHAT THE EARTH WAS LIKE

When dinosaurs lived, the Earth was different than it is today. It was warm almost everywhere. There was a lot of rain. There were jungles filled with tall trees and plants. That meant there was plenty to eat for even the largest plant-eating dinosaur!

It's a Fact!

• Crocodiles were alive at the time of the dinosaurs. Today's crocodiles look a lot like the ones that lived millions of years ago. However, they are much smaller now!

• Scientists who study dinosaurs have discovered more than 600 kinds of dinosaurs. Even more may be discovered in the future.

• There were no flying dinosaurs. Pteranodon, such as the pterodactyl, could fly, but they weren't really dinosaurs. They were another kind of reptile.

The *Garudimimus* lived in Asia. It walked on two legs and had no teeth at all.

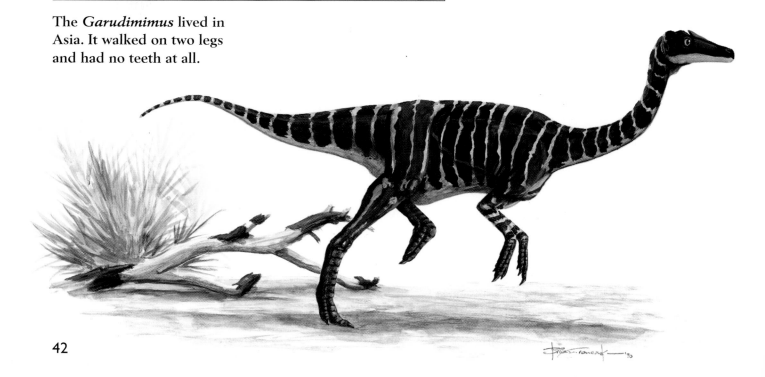

Dinosaur babies came from eggs. The *Saltasaurus* dinosaurs made nests out of dirt for their eggs. The eggs were the size of small soccer balls. The dinosaurs had to watch their eggs closely. Other dinosaurs would try to steal them for food!

Most paleontologists think that dinosaurs were reptiles. Reptiles have tough, scaly skin. Their babies are born from eggs. They have cold blood. Cold-blooded animals have blood that is the same temperature as the air around them.

Scientists who study dinosaurs are called *paleontologists* (pay-lee-uhn-TAH-luh-jists). They search for dinosaur fossils. Paleontologists study fossils to learn what dinosaurs looked like and how they might have acted.

More to Explore

Jobs • Reptiles • Rocks

43

Earth

The Earth is the planet we live on. It is a huge ball that spins around in space. It is one of nine planets that travel around the Sun. The Earth is different from the other planets because it is surrounded by a thick layer of air called the atmosphere. *The atmosphere is what lets us live here. It gives us air to breathe. The surface of the Earth is made up of water, rock, and land.*

This is the Earth as it looks from space. The brown parts are pieces of land. The dark blue parts are the oceans and other water. The white parts are clouds and ice.

STRUCTURE OF THE EARTH

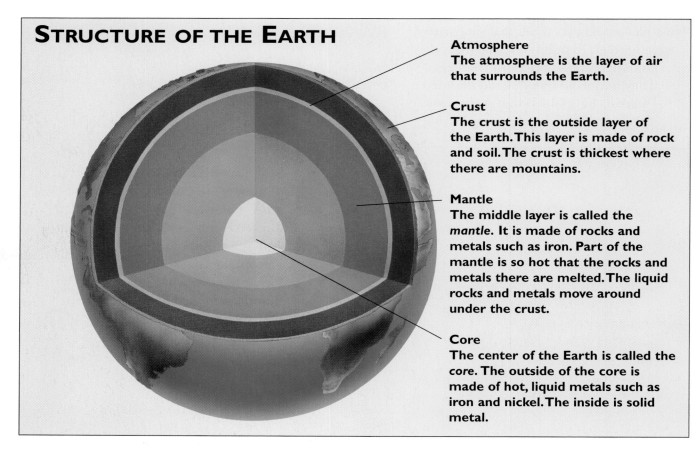

Atmosphere
The atmosphere is the layer of air that surrounds the Earth.

Crust
The crust is the outside layer of the Earth. This layer is made of rock and soil. The crust is thickest where there are mountains.

Mantle
The middle layer is called the *mantle.* It is made of rocks and metals such as iron. Part of the mantle is so hot that the rocks and metals there are melted. The liquid rocks and metals move around under the crust.

Core
The center of the Earth is called the *core.* The outside of the core is made of hot, liquid metals such as iron and nickel. The inside is solid metal.

DAY AND NIGHT

It takes 24 hours for the Earth to spin around once. This movement causes day and night.

It is daylight in places that are turned toward the Sun.

It is night in places that are turned away from the Sun.

Axis

Sun's Rays

3 AM

6 AM

9 AM

Earth's Rotation

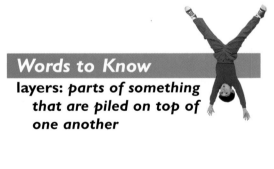

Words to Know

layers: *parts of something that are piled on top of one another*

A volcano happens when melted rock from the mantle comes through an opening in the Earth's crust. The melted rock is called *lava.* The hot lava pours out of a volcano and makes a cone-shape mound that becomes a mountain. When the lava cools, it becomes hard rock. Every time a volcano erupts, new lava makes the mountain even bigger.

The Earth's crust isn't one large piece. It is made of thick slabs called *plates.* The plates float and slowly move on the melted rock of the mantle. Sometimes the plates in one part of the world move quickly. They bump into each other. When that happens, the ground slides and shakes. It is an earthquake!

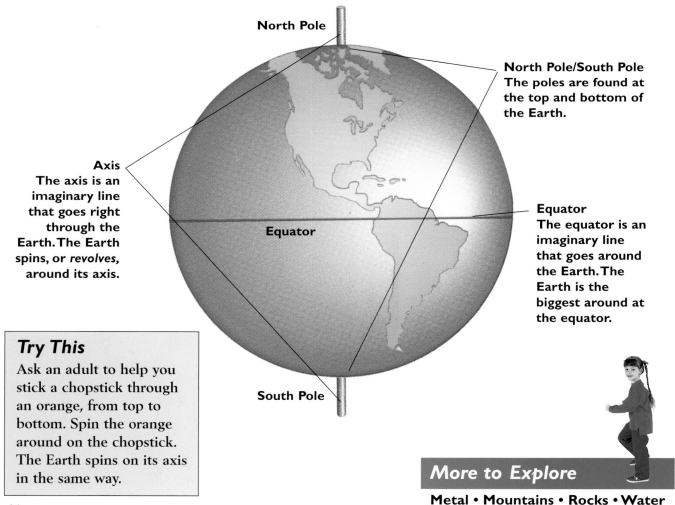

North Pole

North Pole/South Pole
The poles are found at the top and bottom of the Earth.

Axis
The axis is an imaginary line that goes right through the Earth. The Earth spins, or *revolves,* around its axis.

Equator

Equator
The equator is an imaginary line that goes around the Earth. The Earth is the biggest around at the equator.

South Pole

Try This
Ask an adult to help you stick a chopstick through an orange, from top to bottom. Spin the orange around on the chopstick. The Earth spins on its axis in the same way.

More to Explore

Metal • Mountains • Rocks • Water

Electricity

Electricity is a kind of energy that is found in nature. Everything on Earth is made of tiny parts called **atoms***. Atoms contain even tinier parts called* **electrons***. Sometimes these electrons move from one atom to another. That makes electricity.*

Lightning is electricity. During a storm, electrons jump from one cloud to another or from a cloud to the ground. The electricity it causes makes a big spark, which is a bolt of lightning!

Words to Know

energy: the power to do things

Try This

You can create a kind of electricity called *static electricity.* Quickly rub a blown-up balloon against your hair. Then let go. The balloon should stick to your head. Electrons from your hair moved to the balloon!

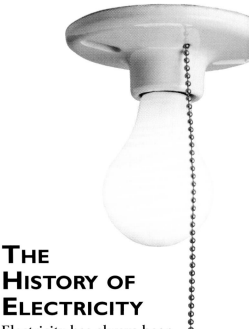

Electricity lets us use lots of things, including lamps, computers, and microwaves. Anything with a plug needs electricity to work. Batteries are also a form of electricity. When a battery is put into a flashlight, an electric current moves from the battery to the bulb of the flashlight and back again. That makes enough energy to light the bulb.

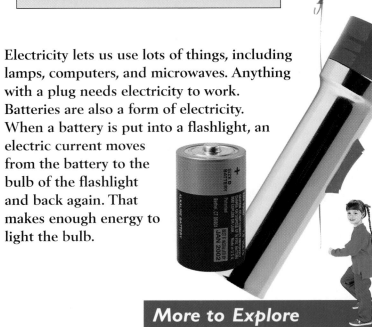

THE HISTORY OF ELECTRICITY

Electricity has always been around, but people haven't always known how to use it. A few hundred years ago, though, scientists started to understand electricity and how it works.

More to Explore

Light • Weather

Endangered Species

Sometimes all the animals of one kind die, or become extinct. Animals that are in danger of becoming extinct are called endangered species. Animals can become endangered for many reasons. They may not have enough room to live and find food. Too many may be killed by hunters. Animals may also die when harmful things get into the water, soil, or air.

Some animals are endangered because they are losing their *habitat.* A habitat is the place where an animal lives, finds food, and has its babies. The Giant Panda has that problem. It only eats bamboo. Now there are not enough bamboo forests left to feed the Giant Pandas.

ENDANGERED PLANTS

Some plants are also endangered, especially in the tropical rain forest. Many trees have been cut down for farming, lumber, and firewood. Many plants that grew in the jungle are now gone.

Sometimes animals are endangered because of pollution. Pollution is when harmful things get into the water, soil, or air. Fish die when bad things get into the water. They can't breathe or find food to eat.

SAVING ANIMALS

People around the world are working hard to save endangered animals. There are many places where animals are protected. People cannot hunt the animals or do anything that might hurt them. These places are called *wildlife preserves* or *animal parks.* Zoos also work to protect animals.

Some people take care of endangered animals that are hurt or that need help. When the animals can care for themselves, they are set free.

Bengal tiger

Ivory-billed woodpecker

Orangutan

Snow leopard

California condor

Sumatran rhinoceros

Europe

Europe is one of the world's seven continents. Europe is connected to Asia, which is another continent. Europe has many different types of land. Some parts have hills and mountains. Other parts are flat and have thick forests. Europe has many important people in the areas of health and education.

The Alps

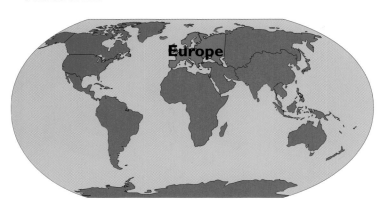

THE LAND

Almost half of Europe is covered with forests. Germany, a country in Europe, has many forests. The Black Forest there got its name because the woods are so thick it looks black inside.

Another big part of Europe is farmland. Some countries there get lots of sun and have good soil to grow crops. In places where it is really warm, such as the country of Greece, they grow olives on farms called *groves.*

Europe is also known for its mountains. The mountains are usually cold, especially in the winter. The Alps are very famous.

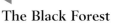

Words to Know

continent: *a large body of land*
culture: *the way of life for a group of people*

The Black Forest

THE PEOPLE

Europe has a long history. Its *culture*, or way of life, has spread to many parts of the world. Across Europe, about 60 different languages are spoken.

Many people in Europe used to live on farms. Most people now live in cities. Many cities in Europe are famous. These cities are popular with tourists. Millions of people visit Europe each year.

Europe has a strong school system. Almost everyone who grows up there knows how to read. This is different from some other places, where not everyone goes to school.

WILDLIFE

The forests of Europe are home to many plants and animals. The brown bear likes to live in forests. It is found all over Europe in wooded areas. Brown bears are good hunters, but they eat mostly plants.

Reindeer live in the colder parts of Europe. They are very important to some groups of people there. These people use the animals for food and their skins for shelter and clothing. Some even ride the reindeer to get around!

Brown bear

Reindeer

◄

Europe contains some of the most famous buildings and structures, including many old churches and castles. The Eiffel Tower in Paris, France, is a structure known all over the world.

More to Explore

Buildings • Forest • Mountains

Explorers

An explorer is a person who travels to an unknown place. Since long ago, explorers have tried to visit far-off places. Explorers often were trying to find new lands or new goods to trade. Sometimes explorers were just looking for adventure! People still explore places for those same reasons.

More to Explore

Asia • Europe • Inventions • North America • Oceans • Space

Sometimes explorers get lucky. Christopher Columbus was an explorer. He was trying to go to India, but he got lost. Instead he landed in what is now called North America!

Explorers bring back information about the places they visit. For example, long ago people in Europe didn't know much about the country of China. A man named Marco Polo explored China. He found the country had lots of interesting things, such as inventions and beautiful kinds of cloth. He brought back some new things for people in Europe to try.

People go into space to explore the big universe.

TODAY'S EXPLORATIONS

Over thousands of years, most of the Earth has been explored. But explorers are still searching for new places to discover! Scientists use technology to explore areas that were impossible to reach before. The deepest parts of the ocean and outer space are the new frontiers.

Family

A family is a group of people who are related to one another. There are many different kinds and sizes of families. Some families may have one parent and one child. Other families may have two parents and many children. Every family is part of an even larger family that includes grandparents, aunts, uncles, and cousins.

Many families like to eat together. This helps them spend time with each other.

A marriage happens when a person takes a husband or wife. A person gets married in what is called a wedding ceremony. These ceremonies are different all around the world.

A family grows as children come into the family. Children can be born into the family. They can also be adopted into a family.

More to Explore

Holidays • Homes

Farms

Farms are places where plants or animals are raised to be used for food or to make other products. Plants that are grown on farms are called crops. Animals that are raised for food are called livestock. Farming is very important. Without farms, people would not have enough food to eat.

Machines make farming easier, but they can't do everything. Farmers still have to do some work by hand. Other farmers don't have money for machines. They do all of the work by hand.

Pineapple fields

Rice fields

KINDS OF FARMS

There are many different kinds of farms. Farmers have to think about the land and the weather when they decide what kind of crops or animals they will raise. Some crops, such as pineapples or bananas, only grow where it is hot all the time. Grains such as wheat and corn grow well in places that have rich soil, cool winters, and warm summers.

Some crops need a lot of water. Rice grows in shallow water. Rice farmers usually live where there is a lot of rain.

Goat

Chicken

Pig

Many animals that are raised for food need a lot of space so they have enough grass or grains to eat. The people on this ranch in Australia raise sheep.

FARM MACHINES

Farming is easier today than it was hundreds of years ago. There are machines that do much of the work. Farmers use machines to dig up the soil, plant seeds, remove weeds, and water their fields. They even use machines to pick the crops when they are ripe.

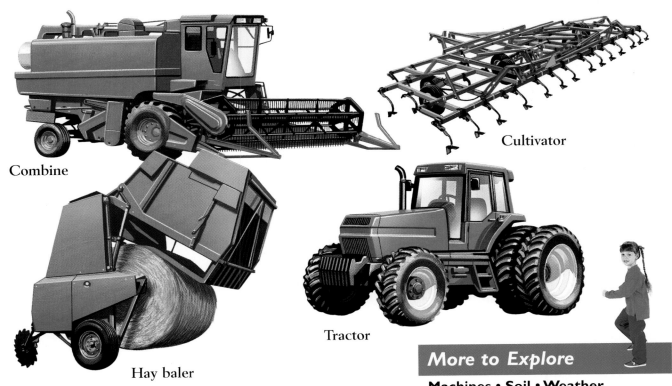

Combine

Cultivator

Hay baler

Tractor

More to Explore

Machines • Soil • Weather

Fish

Fish are animals that live in water, such as the ocean or lakes and streams. They move by swimming, and breathe with gills that take oxygen from the water. Most fish are covered with scales. They are cold-blooded, which means their blood is the same temperature as the water around them.

Salmon live in the oceans. But when it is time to have babies, these fish swim back to the rivers or streams where they were born. They lay their eggs there. When the young fish are strong enough, they swim to the ocean. Later, they come back to the same river or stream to lay eggs. Scientists don't understand exactly how the salmon know where to go!

Words to Know

female: *an animal that can become a mother*
male: *an animal that can become a father*
oxygen: *a gas that animals need to breathe in order to live*

A HORSE THAT IS A FISH

The sea horse isn't shaped like most fish. Its curved neck and long nose make it look like a tiny horse. The sea horse swims by moving its tail, but its body stays up so it looks like it is standing. The sea horse wraps its tail around a piece of seaweed when it wants to rest.

Even the way this fish has babies is different. The female sea horse lays eggs in a pouch on the male sea horse's body. The male takes care of the eggs until the tiny sea horses hatch!

THE PARTS OF A FISH

Fish have a few special parts that help them live in the water. For example, fish breathe by opening their mouths and taking in water. The water travels over the gills, where oxygen gets taken out and sent into the fish's blood. The leftover water gets squirted out of the fish's body.

Most fish swim by wiggling the tail fin from side to side. Many fish also have an air-filled bag in their bodies. This bag is called a *swim bladder*. The air in the swim bladder helps fish float and keeps them from tipping over.

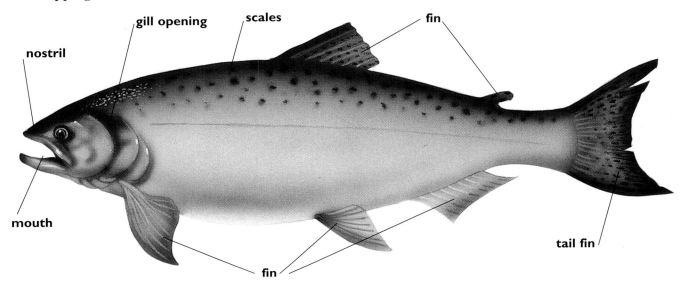

gill opening   scales   fin

nostril

mouth

fin

tail fin

It's a Fact!
• The lungfish has both gills and lungs. It comes to the surface of the water to breathe. This fish can even stay on land for a while.
• Eels are bony fish that look a little like snakes. They have long, thin bodies and no tail fin. Eels move by wiggling their bodies back and forth.

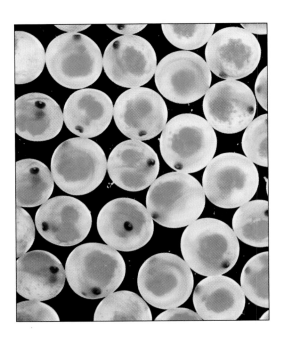

Most baby fish hatch from eggs. A female fish lays hundreds or thousands of eggs at once. The eggs are not covered with a hard shell. They are soft and are usually in a large clump. Most fish do not take care of their young. When the eggs hatch, the young fish are ready to take care of themselves.

More to Explore

Lakes and Ponds • Ocean • Rivers and Streams

Flags

A flag is a piece of cloth sewn with patterns of colors or special designs. A flag is a symbol for a country or a group such as a company or club. Flags help people show honor and respect. In the United States, each state also has its own flag. National and state flags are often flown at schools and government buildings.

There are lots of different flags! Each country in the world has a special one of its own.

Flags can have special names. The U.S. flag, for example, is often called "The Stars and Stripes." The symbols on flags may remind people of history. The 50 stars on the American flag stand for each state in the country. The stripes stand for the original 13 states when the country first started.

Some groups have their own flags. The Red Cross is a group that helps all kinds of people. When you see a place with this flag, you know you can find help there.

Countries also have flags. Countries use flags to tell who they are and to show pride. This is the Canadian flag. When you see it, you think of the country of Canada.

Food

Food is what you eat or drink. Your body uses food for energy. Food helps you grow strong and stay healthy. Food also gives your body the energy it needs to keep working.

WHERE FOOD COMES FROM

Your family probably gets most of its food from the grocery store. But where does food come from before it reaches the store? A lot of the food you eat comes from plants that farmers raise. Some plants, like beans, corn, and tomatoes, go to stores to be sold after they are picked.

Other plants go to factories that turn them into food. For example, corn and wheat are made into cereal. The cereal is put into boxes or bags, and then it goes to the grocery store so people can buy it.

FOOD AROUND THE WORLD

People around the world eat different foods. This is partly because they have different ideas about what tastes good. You probably wouldn't want to eat an insect. But in some parts of the world, a crunchy bug is a favorite treat!

People also eat different foods because they are easier to grow or buy in some places than they are in others. People who live where it is warm all year eat a lot of fruit because it grows well in warm places. People who live near water often eat a lot of fish.

People in Africa might eat food that looks a little bit different from what you're used to.

PYRAMID POWER!

There are six different groups of foods. Each food group is important. Each helps your body in different ways. To stay healthy, you must eat a balanced diet. That means eating the right amounts of food from each food group. The Food Pyramid shows what you should eat every day.

Try This

Make a list to keep track of everything you eat and drink for one day. Then look at the Food Pyramid again. Did you eat the right amount of food from each food group?

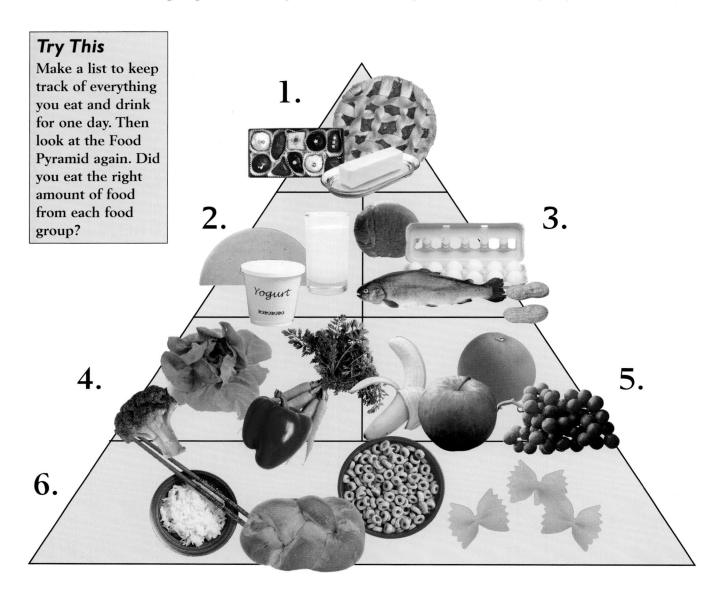

1. Fats, Oils, and Sugar Group
Eat only a little of these foods each day.

2. Milk, Yogurt, and Cheese Group
Eat two to three servings each day. Choose products that are low in fat.

3. Meat, Poultry, Fish, Beans, Eggs, and Nuts Group
Eat two to three servings each day.

4. Vegetable Group
Eat three to five servings each day.

5. Fruit Group
Eat two to four servings each day.

6. Bread, Cereal, Rice, and Pasta Group
Eat six to eleven servings each day. Choose healthful whole grains.

Milk and the foods that are made from milk are called *dairy products.* Dairy products are important because they have a nutrient called *calcium.* Your body uses calcium to build strong bones and teeth. To get enough, you should drink milk and eat foods such as cheese and yogurt.

It's a Fact!

Did you ever hear the saying "An apple a day keeps the doctor away"? Apples are full of vitamins and other nutrients that are good for you. So eating foods such as apples helps to keep you healthy. And that keeps the doctor away!

KNOW YOUR NUTRIENTS

Nutrients are the parts of food that help you grow and stay healthy. Vitamins are one important kind of nutrient. Different vitamins help the body in different ways. Your body gets most of the vitamins it needs from the food you eat. Some people also take vitamin pills to be sure they get enough of every vitamin.

VITAMIN	WHAT IT DOES	WHERE IT IS FOUND
A	keeps your eyes healthy	eggs, whole milk, liver
B	helps your blood, skin, and hair	meat, fish, cereal, eggs
C	fights colds and infections	oranges, lemons, other fruits
D	makes bones and teeth strong	fish, added to milk
E	keeps blood healthy and fights disease	liver, cereal, cabbage
K	makes cuts stop bleeding	green vegetables, liver, eggs

More to Explore

The Body • Farms • Health • Plants

Forest

An area of land that has many trees growing close together is called a forest. Forests are found everywhere in the world except where the land is always frozen. A forest has layers. The tallest trees form the top layer. Shorter trees, bushes, and shrubs grow in the middle layer. Mosses, ferns, and small plants grow on the bottom layer.

Rain forests grow where there is a lot of rain. Some rain forests grow where it is always cool. Some grow where it is hot. They are also called *jungles.*

A deciduous (di-SI-joo-wuhs) forest grows in places that have cool winters, warm summers, and rain or snow all year long. The trees lose their leaves in the fall. New leaves grow back in the spring.

Coniferous (koh-NIH-fuh-ruhs) forests grow where there are long, cold winters. Most of the trees there are conifers. They have needlelike leaves that do not fall off in the autumn.

A mixed forest has deciduous trees and conifers. This forest grows where it is warm enough for deciduous trees and cool enough for conifers.

More to Explore

Plants • Trees • Weather

Grasslands

Grasslands are areas where most of the land is covered by grassy plants. Grasslands grow where there is not enough rain for forests but too much rain to be a desert. The land may be flat or having rolling hills.

Some grasslands are called *natural grasslands.* That means they have always been covered with grasses. Some grasslands were once covered with trees. They became grasslands when people cut the trees down for farmland or to build houses.

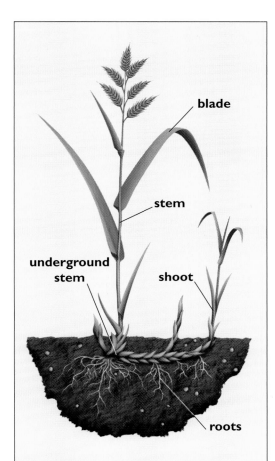

PARTS OF GRASS

Grasses are plants with thin, hollow stems. They have straight, narrow leaves called *blades.* The roots of grasses send out underground stems. New grasses that grow from these stems are called *shoots.*

There are many kinds of grass. Each kind grows to a different height. Elephant grass grows in Africa. It can be 13 feet tall! Animals can hide in there easily.

More to Explore

Africa • Plants

63

Health

Health means keeping your body safe from disease and other things that can harm it. To stay healthy, you must eat the right foods and get plenty of sleep and exercise. You must also take good care of your eyes, ears, teeth, and other parts of your body. When you are sick, you are not healthy. Taking medicine or visiting a doctor can help you become healthy again.

Exercise can help keep you healthy! You should try to stay active to keep your body strong and fit.

Words to Know

microscope: *a machine that makes small objects look larger*

SLEEP

To stay healthy, you need to get the right amount of sleep. Grown-ups need about eight hours of sleep a day. Children need between 10 and 12 hours of sleep. And small babies sleep most of the day and night!

When you sleep, your body gets to rest. Your heart keeps on beating, but it doesn't have to beat as fast. Your lungs keep working so you can breathe, but they don't have to work as hard as they do when you are awake.

Try This

Take your pulse. Gently press two fingers from one hand against the inside of the other wrist. You should be able to feel your pulse, which is your heartbeat. Ask someone to time you for one minute as you count the number of heartbeats. A healthy person usually has a pulse between 60 and 100 beats per minute.

Staying Healthy

Long ago, many people died from diseases such as measles. Today there are medicines called *vaccines* (vak-SEENS) that keep people from getting some diseases. Doctors give young children vaccines. These help kids stay healthy. Some vaccines are given as shots. Others are taken as liquid medicine or pills.

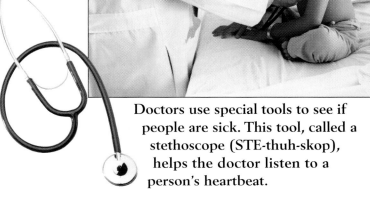

Doctors use special tools to see if people are sick. This tool, called a stethoscope (STE-thuh-skop), helps the doctor listen to a person's heartbeat.

Germs

Germs are creatures that are so tiny they can only be seen with a microscope. When germs get inside your body, they can make you sick. Germs can also spread from one person to another.

To keep germs from making you sick, be sure to follow these health rules:

- Wash your hands before and after you eat.
- Wash your hands after you go to the bathroom.
- Use a handkerchief or tissue when you cough or sneeze.
- Try not to touch things that a sick person has touched.

EATING WELL

The food you eat helps your body grow strong. It also helps you stay healthy. If you do not eat the right foods, you can get sick.

Every day you should eat:

Two or three servings of low-fat dairy products

Five to eight servings of fruits and vegetables

Apples

Green salad

Milk

Cheese

Five to eleven servings of whole-grain bread, cereal, rice, or pasta

Two or three servings of meat, fish, beans, eggs, or nuts

Cereal

Bread

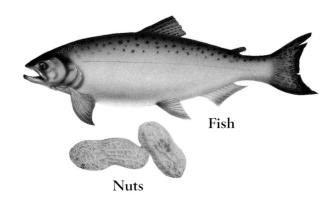

Fish

Nuts

66

YOUR TEETH

You are lucky to have two sets of teeth. Your first teeth are called *baby teeth.* You probably started getting baby teeth when you were about six months old. You have 20 baby teeth in all.

When you are about six years old, your second set of teeth start growing. These are called your *permanent teeth.* Your permanent teeth push your baby teeth out of the way and make them fall out. By the time you are grown up, you will have 32 permanent teeth.

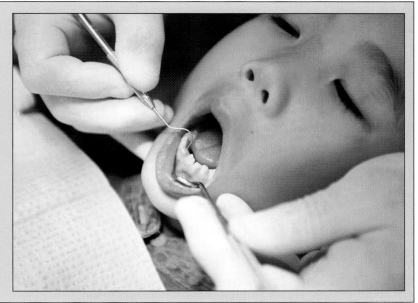

TAKING CARE OF YOUR TEETH

Part of staying healthy is taking care of your teeth. Sugar in the food you eat can make holes in your teeth. These holes are called *cavities.* Here are some ways you can keep cavities from happening to you!

- Try not to eat too many sugary foods.
- Brush your teeth after every meal.
- Visit the dentist twice a year.
- Drink milk and eat foods with lots of calcium, such as cheese and yogurt. Calcium helps make your teeth strong!

It's a Fact!

- When you are healthy, your body's temperature is 98.6 degrees. If your temperature gets higher than that, you have a fever. A fever means your body is busy fighting germs.
- Sneezing doesn't always mean you are sick with a cold. It is a way to get rid of things that don't belong inside your body. For example, when you breathe in dust, a big sneeze blows the dust back out!

Sunscreen can keep you from being hurt by the sun. You should always wear it. You should also try to stay out of the sun during the middle of the day. If you do have to be in the sun, you should wear sunglasses and a hat.

More to Explore

The Body • Food

Holidays

The word holiday comes from the words "holy day." These days were set apart from the usual days of work and rest. Sometimes holidays are for praying or worshiping. Other times, holidays have to do with special days for a country. On holidays, people celebrate or honor a person or a set of beliefs. People around the world celebrate different holidays.

In the United States and Canada, families celebrate a day of Thanksgiving with feasts. This is a fall tradition that has been around for hundreds of years.

It's a Fact!
• Some countries, such as Japan and Turkey, have a holiday that celebrates children.
• Many countries celebrate a National Day or Independence Day to honor their history.

Hanukkah

Christmas

NORTH AMERICAN HOLIDAYS

People in North America celebrate many different holidays. Some of these holidays, such as Christmas, Passover, or Ramadan, are religious. Only people of certain religions celebrate these holidays.

Some holidays are celebrated by lots of people, no matter what their religion. Almost everyone in the United States celebrates Independence Day, for example. This is like a birthday celebration for the country!

The Kandy Esala Perahera is the one of the biggest holidays in the country of Sri Lanka. It takes place in July or August. Elephants, dancers, and acrobats are all part of the celebration.

Spring celebrations honor the coming of spring. Holi is celebrated in the spring in the country of India. Holi is sometimes called "the festival of colors." People celebrate with bright powders and paints and lots of singing and dancing.

HOLIDAY CALENDARS

Some holidays are celebrated on the same date each year. The dates of other holidays sometimes move. They might be based on a day of the week, such as the last Thursday of a certain month. Or the date might depend on the moon or on a religious calendar.

Some African Americans celebrate Kwanza in the winter. Kwanza is a week of celebrating African history and culture.

More to Explore

Family • North America • Religion • The Seasons

Homes

The place a person lives is his or her home. Homes provide shelter. A shelter is a place that protects people from rain, snow, cold, wind, and heat. Everyone needs a home of some type. All homes do not look the same, though. They are different all around the world.

Homes are places where people eat, sleep, and spend time with those they love.

HOMES BUILT FOR WEATHER

People build their houses so they work best for the weather around them. In desert places, people build their homes very close together. This way, more of the home is protected from the hot sun.

In places with a lot of snow, houses have steep roofs. This stops too much snow from gathering on top of the house.

Homes around the world are built out of different materials. People use what is found in their area. The American Indians in the southwestern United States, for example, used *adobe*. Adobe is a mixture of clay, sand, and straw. It kept the building cool even when the sun was very hot.

KINDS OF HOMES

Think about your home. Does it look the same as all the other homes you've seen? Probably not. There are lots of different types of homes. Some people live in buildings that have more than one home inside. These are called *apartments.* Some people live in homes that can be moved around easily. These are called *mobile homes.*

People all over the world live in different kinds of homes. People who live near rivers on the island of Borneo live in buildings called *longhouses.* Many families live in one longhouse. Each family gets a room inside the building.

PARTS OF A HOME

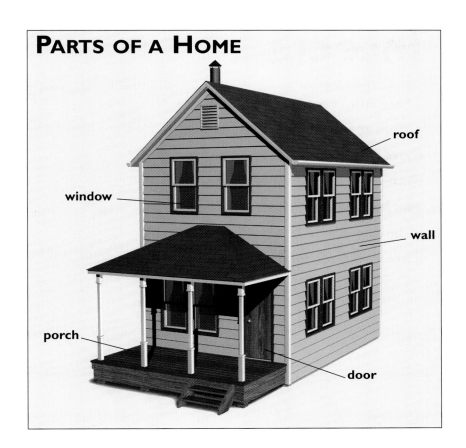

roof

window

wall

porch

door

Japanese gassho house

Bornean longhouse

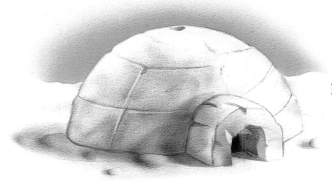

Eskimo igloo

More to Explore

Buildings • Construction • Family

71

Insects

There are more than a million different kinds of insects. In fact, there are more insects on Earth than any other animal. Insects can be found everywhere, even in places where the land is frozen all year long.

It's a Fact!

• Spiders are not insects. They have two body parts and eight legs. Insects have three body parts and six legs.

• Termites have an unusual diet. They eat wood.

When some insects hatch, they look a lot like their parents. These young insects are called *nymphs.* They do not go through metamorphosis, but they do grow and change. An insect's skin is too hard to grow. When the insect gets too big, the skin splits. The insect sheds the old skin and comes out with a new, larger skin. Dragonflies and locusts grow like this.

THE WAY SOME INSECTS GROW

Young insects hatch from eggs laid by a female insect. Many young insects don't look like their parents. Instead they are called *larva* (LAHR-vuh) and look like fat worms with legs.

These insects go through stages to become adults. First the insect is an egg and then a larva. Next it becomes something called a *pupa* (PYOO-puh). And finally, it becomes an adult. These stages are called *metamorphosis* (meh-tuh-MOR-fuh-sus).

A caterpillar is the larva of a butterfly. This insect goes through metamorphosis as it becomes an adult butterfly.

1. The caterpillar is a larva of a butterfly.

2. The caterpillar makes a case called a *chrysalis* (KRI-suh-luhs). Inside the chrysalis, it rests and changes. This is the butterfly's pupa stage.

3. A butterfly comes out of the chrysalis.

THE PARTS OF AN INSECT

All adult insects have bodies with three parts. The three parts of an adult insect's body are the head, thorax, and abdomen. They also have wings, six legs, and a pair of feelers called *antennae* (an-TE-nuh). They also have a hard skin.

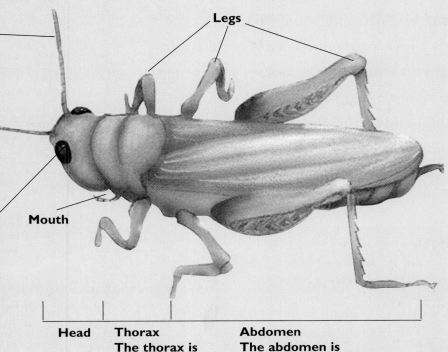

Antennae
Two antennae stick out at the front of an insect's head. Antennae are sometimes called *feelers* because the insect uses them for feeling. Antennae are also used to taste and smell things.

Eye
Insects have unusual eyes. Each eye is made up of many parts. Each of the parts sees the same thing. When a human would see only one apple, an insect would see hundreds of apples!

Legs

Mouth

Head

Thorax
The thorax is the middle section of an insect's body.

Abdomen
The abdomen is the hind part of an insect. It is the largest part, too.

KINDS OF BEES

Queen bee   Drone   Worker

Try This
Push your fingertips gently against the skin on your arm. Now press your fingertips against a fingernail. Can you feel the difference? An insect's body has a hard covering that is a little like your fingernail. It protects the insect's body.

More to Explore

Life Cycle • Spiders

Inventions

An invention is something that has been invented, or made for the first time. An invention can be a machine or a way of doing things. Inventions often make something better. Inventions sometimes change people's lives.

Some inventions are created by accident. The inventors were trying to do something else but found an invention instead. The medicine penicillin was invented by accident. We should be glad. Penicillin has saved millions of lives!

Inventions can change the world! Someone long, long ago invented the wheel. It helped people move things more easily. Think how much we still use the wheel today!

The television is definitely a popular invention! The first TVs could not show colors. All of the shows were in black and white.

TYPES OF INVENTIONS

Communication inventions help people talk to each other. They also help people get information. The phone is an invention.

Transportation inventions help us travel from one place to another. Cars and bikes are inventions.

Inventions for health help cure illness and keep people well. The stethescope (STE-thuh-skohp) is an invention.

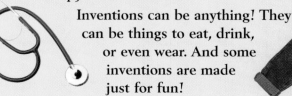

Inventions can be anything! They can be things to eat, drink, or even wear. And some inventions are made just for fun!

Jobs

People all over the world do different kinds of work. They earn money from their jobs to pay for homes, food, clothes, and other things they need. There are hundreds of different kinds of jobs.

Teachers help students study and learn.

Farmers grow crops and raise animals. Farming is an important job all over the world.

Builders make homes, buildings, roads, and other structures.

Workers such as firefighters and police officers help keep places safe.

People who work in factories help create things to sell.

TOOLS WORKERS USE

Workers often need special tools to do their jobs. A person who works in construction might use a bulldozer. A businessperson probably uses a computer. Tools can really make a person's job easier to do!

More to Explore

Business • Construction • Farms • Machines • Rescue

Lakes and Ponds

A lake is a large hollow space in the land that is filled with water. Every lake must always take in more water, or it will dry up. Rain, rivers, and streams provide this water. A pond is like a lake, but it is smaller. Because they are large, lakes can have waves. The water in ponds is still, or doesn't move.

Most of the Earth's water is in oceans. Ocean water is saltwater. Animals and plants cannot drink saltwater. Lakes have freshwater. This water can be drunk. It can also be used to help crops grow.

It is important to take care of our lakes. If chemicals or other bad things get into a lake, the water will not be safe to use. Most places have laws to keep bad things from getting into lake water.

LAKE AND POND ANIMALS

Lakes and ponds are home to many animals. Birds like ducks and geese love to swim in the water there. Many different kinds of fish live in the water, too. There are also lots of frogs and snakes and turtles living near the water.

There are many fun things to do on a lake. People can use lakes for swimming, boating, fishing, and lots of other activities.

More to Explore

Birds • Fish • Ocean • Plants • Rivers and Streams • Water

Language

A language is a set of sounds and signs that people use to communicate with one another. Languages can be spoken or written. Throughout the world, people use thousands of different languages. English is an example of one type of language.

Language can be written, such as in a book, or it can be spoken, such as when you talk.

Written languages often use letters. Some languages use characters or even pictures instead of letters!

Not every language looks like English. Some languages, such as Greek, use other types of letters.

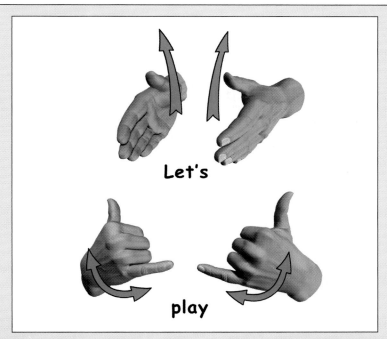

Let's

play

This is how to say "Let's play!" in American Sign Language. To say *Let's,* hold your hands so that they face each other. Then move them up and out. Then hold your hands as shown to say *play.* Shake them back and forth.

SIGN LANGUAGE

Sign language is a way of communicating. People who cannot hear or speak often use sign language. There are signs for letters so people can spell words. There are also signs that stand for whole words. There are different systems of sign language used around the world.

Life Cycle

Every living thing goes through stages in its life. The seeds of plants sprout, become grown plants, make seeds of their own, and later die. Animals are born, grow to become adults, have babies of their own, become old, and die. These stages in the life of a plant or animal are called its life cycle.

An egg is the first stage in the life cycle of many animals. Insects, fish, amphibians, reptiles, birds, and other animals lay eggs. The eggs usually have a tough covering called a *shell*. The baby animals break out of the eggs, or *hatch*.

A MAMMAL LIFE CYCLE

Mammals start out as eggs, too. But mammal eggs do not have shells. The eggs grow inside the mother's body until the baby animal is born.

1. A kitten starts as an egg that grows inside the mother cat's body.
2. The kitten is born. The mother cat feeds and takes care of the kitten.
3. The kitten grows larger and learns to care for itself.
4. The kitten becomes an adult cat. If it is a female, it can have kittens of its own.

A PLANT LIFE CYCLE

A seed is the first stage in the life cycle of most plants. The seed grows into an adult plant that makes seeds for new plants of the same kind.

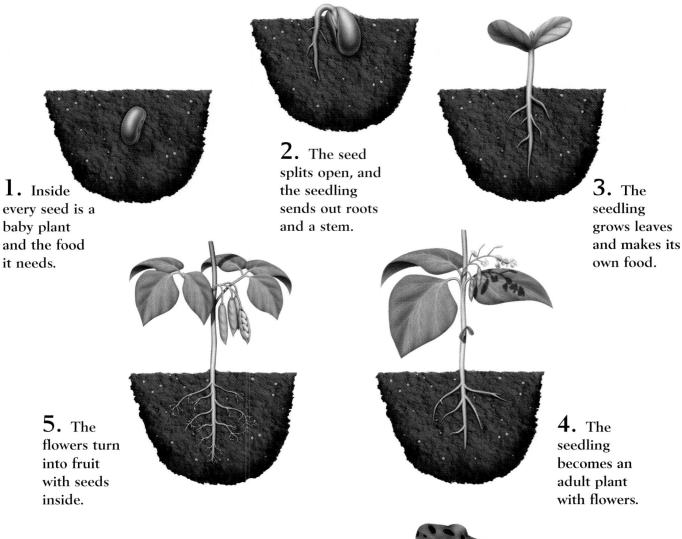

1. Inside every seed is a baby plant and the food it needs.

2. The seed splits open, and the seedling sends out roots and a stem.

3. The seedling grows leaves and makes its own food.

5. The flowers turn into fruit with seeds inside.

4. The seedling becomes an adult plant with flowers.

Some baby insects and amphibians do not look like their parents. They have some unusual stages in their life cycles. During these stages, they change completely. This is called *metamorphosis* (meh-tuh-MOR-fuh-suhs). For example, a frog egg turns into a tadpole. As it grows, the tadpole gets legs and a tail. Then the tadpole becomes a frog.

Words to Know

cycle: *something that happens over and over again in the same way*

More to Explore

Amphibians • Birds • Fish • Insect • Mammals • Plants • Reptiles

Light

Light is a form of energy. It travels in invisible waves through water, air, and empty space. Light waves can even travel through some objects. Light moves faster than anything else on Earth or in space. Light waves from the sun travel 93 million miles to reach Earth. They make the trip in about eight minutes!

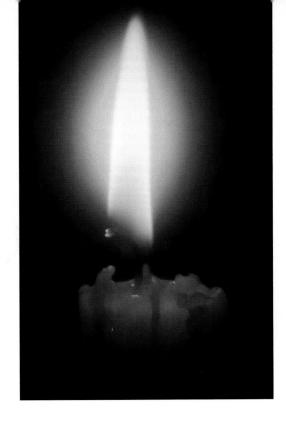

Heat and light go together. The sun and other stars shine because of fiery gases. A candle gives off light from the fire of its burning wick. Even a lightbulb uses heat to make light. When electricity flows through a thin wire inside a light-bulb, the wire heats up. The glow of the hot wire is what makes light.

Words to Know

indigo: *a dark blue–purple color*
violet: *a light purple color*

Light may look clear, but it is made up of seven colors: red, orange, yellow, green, blue, indigo, and violet. When light hits an object, some colors bounce back, or *reflect*. The colors you see are the ones that reflect.

As light moves through space and air, it hits objects. Light acts in different ways depending on what it hits.

Light travels through some objects. Things that light shines through are called *transparent* (trans-PAR-uhnt).

Sometimes only part of the light can pass through an object. Things that let some light through are called *translucent* (trans-LOO-suhnt).

Objects that light cannot travel through are called *opaque* (oh-PAYK).

Transparent

Translucent

Opaque

More to Explore

Colors • Electricity • The Senses

80

Machines

A machine is something that helps people do a job. Machines can be very simple. A wheel is a machine. But other machines are not simple at all. A car is also a machine.

All the things that help us get from place to place are machines, from the simplest bicycle to the most advanced aircraft. Cars, buses, trucks, and trains are machines with many moving parts.

MACHINES AT WORK

You can see many machines at places people work. At a construction site, you can see some of the biggest machines, such as cranes and bulldozers. On farms, you can see machines such as tractors and reapers. In factories, machines are used on assembly lines. In offices, people use machines such as copy machines and calculators. And in stores and restaurants, people use cash register machines.

MACHINES IN THE HOME

There is lots of work to be done in a home, and machines are on the job! Most homes use many machines, like the refrigerator, vacuum cleaner, and washer. If there's a yard, many homeowners also use machines such as a lawn mower. All of these machines have many moving parts.

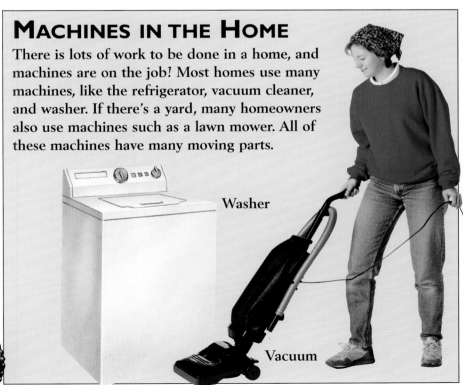

Washer

Vacuum

SIMPLE MACHINES

All machines work with *force*, or a push or a pull, and *motion*, or movement. Simple machines use force and motion to make many things easier to do. Simple machines make it easier to lift heavy things, for example. They also make it easier to move big and heavy things around.

Simple machines have been used for thousands of years. They are all around us still today. There are six kinds of simple machines:

- a pulley
- a wheel and axle
- an inclined plane
- a screw
- a wedge
- a lever

A pulley is a wheel with a rope or chain moving over it.

A screw is an inclined plane that has been wound around a post.

Axle

Wheel

WORKING TOGETHER

Some simple machines are combined to make other simple machines. For example, a pulley uses a wheel to work. And a wedge is made up of two inclined planes working together.

A wheel turns around an axle. Together, they make moving things easier.

An inclined plane is a tilted surface that helps move heavy objects. A ramp is a type of inclined plane.

A wedge is two inclined planes put together. Its force can help to split things easily.

A lever helps direct force. A bottle opener is a type of lever.

It's a Fact!

A car is a moving machine that has about 15,000 parts. Most of these parts are made by other machines! Some of the parts are also put into the car using a machine.

More to Explore

Aircraft • Bicycles • Cars • Computers • Construction • Farms

Magnet

A magnet is a piece of metal that has a special field, called a magnetic field, around it. Having a magnetic field means there are forces around the object that push things away or pull them closer. These forces are felt at the magnetic poles, or the ends of the magnet. Magnets have a north pole and a south pole.

The magnetic field around the Earth's poles can create a colorful show. Tiny bits of material from the sun are attracted toward the poles. As they speed through the air that is all around the Earth, these bits make bands of colors in the night sky. These colors are called *auroras* (uh-ROR-uhs).

A compass (KUHM-puhs) is a needle-shape magnet. It is attracted to the nearest magnetic pole of the Earth. When you hold a compass, the needle will turn until it points to a magnetic pole. The markings on the compass show you which way is north. A compass helps people keep from getting lost.

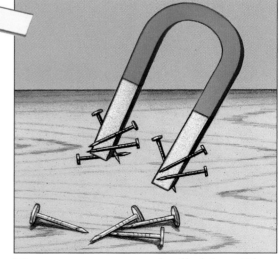

Magnets attract a metal called *iron.* That means that a magnet pulls iron toward itself. Magnets will also attract steel because it is made from iron and other metals. Some other metals, such as aluminum, are not attracted to magnets.

Words to Know
attract: *move toward*
repel: *move away from*

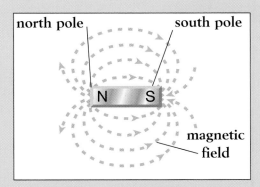

north pole　　　south pole

N　S

magnetic field

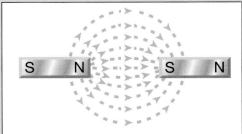

S　N　　　S　N

Unlike magnetic poles attract one another.

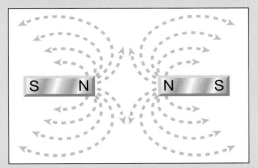

S　N　　　N　S

Like magnetic poles repel one another.

How Magnets Work

If you put two magnets near each other, you can feel the forces they create. When the north pole of one magnet faces the south pole of the other magnet, they are pulled closer. We say that unlike poles *attract* each other.

When the north poles are facing, the magnets push away from each other. We say that like poles *repel* each other.

How Magnets Were Discovered

Thousands of years ago, people discovered that a black stone acted different than other stones. It pulled things that were made of iron toward itself. When two stones of this kind were close, they attracted or repelled each other. This kind of stone is called a *magnet.*

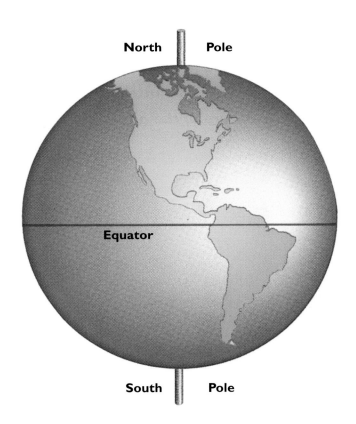

North　Pole

Equator

South　Pole

The Earth has a magnetic field. Like any other object that is magnetic, that means it has two magnetic poles. The magnetic poles are close to the North Pole and South Pole.

More to Explore

Earth • Metal • Rocks

Mammals

Mammals are the only animals that have hair or fur. Young mammals nurse, or drink milk from their mothers' bodies. Mammals protect and care for their young until the babies can survive on their own. All mammals are warm-blooded. That means their blood stays at the same temperature no matter what the temperature of the air around them is.

All mammals breathe air—even mammals that spend their lives in the water. Whales have to come to the surface of the water to breathe. They take in a lot of air at one time. Then they store the air in their huge lungs. A whale can store enough air to stay underwater for two hours!

PRIMATES

People, gorillas, monkeys, and chimpanzees belong to a group of mammals called *primates.* Primates have hands with thumbs that they can use to pick up and hold on to objects. Like people, chimpanzees use their hands to hold and work with tools. They poke sticks into anthills, then pull them out and eat the ants that crawled onto the stick.

Marsupials are a special group of mammals that carry their young in a pouch. A baby kangaroo stays inside its mother's pouch after it is born. It can come out of the pouch when it gets bigger, but it hops back in when it wants to eat or sleep.

WHERE MAMMALS LIVE

Mammals can be found everywhere on Earth. Some types of mammals and the places they live are:

WETLANDS
Beaver

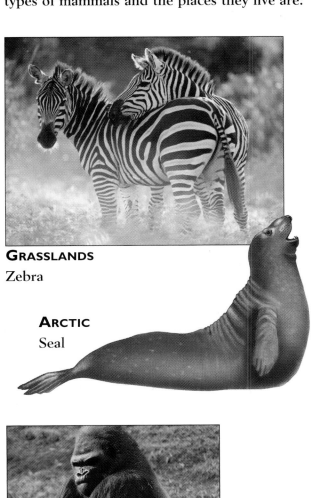

GRASSLANDS
Zebra

UNDERGROUND
Prairie dog

ARCTIC
Seal

RAIN FOREST
Jaguar

MOUNTAINS
Gorilla

OCEAN
Dolphin

FOREST
Deer

Words to Know
communicate: *share thoughts or information*
pouch: *something shaped like a bag*

87

It's a Fact!

Mammals are the largest animals in the world. The elephant is the largest animal that lives on land. The blue whale is the largest animal that lives in water.

It's a Fact!

Mammals have large brains that help them learn and remember. Scientists have even taught some gorillas how to communicate in sign language.

Humans are mammals, too! Think about the hair you have on your body. That's just one of the things that makes you a mammal!

More to Explore

Arctic • Forest • Grasslands • Mountains • Ocean • Wetlands

Maps

A map is a drawing that shows a detailed part of the Earth's surface. People can use a map of the world to find continents and oceans. People can use a map of a particular area to find their way from one place to another.

In early times, people did not travel much. They only knew about things that were near to them. Before the whole Earth could be mapped, people had to discover all the lands.

Some maps show big areas of land from very far away. These maps, such as this one of the United States, don't show a lot of details. People could use it to learn about the whole continent of North America.

It's a Fact!
- Not all maps are flat. A globe is a kind of map. It shows that the world is round.
- Many maps today are made based on pictures taken from outer space.

Some maps show smaller areas like just one specific city. This map of the city of Chicago shows street names and a lake. People could use it to find out how to get around the city.

Mass Media

Newspapers, magazines, radio, television, and the Internet bring people information. These sources of information are called the mass media. *The media share news as well as provide entertainment.*

The average American watches more than four hours of TV every day. That adds up to two whole months out of the year!

RADIO

You probably think of music when you think of the radio. There are many other types of radio shows, though! Some radio programs tell the news and talk with guests and radio listeners.

In fact, radio used to have lots of different shows back before TV was invented. People would gather around the radio and listen to their favorite shows—just like we do today with TV.

INTERNET

The Internet is a network of computers hooked up together. It can provide information, news, and entertainment. Many newspapers, magazines, and television shows have Web sites on the Internet.

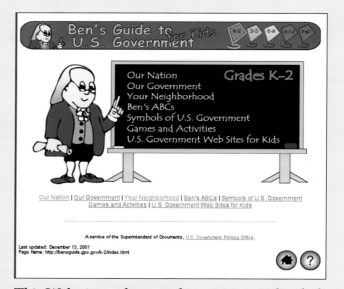

This Web site, at bensguide.gpo.gov, teaches kids about the U.S. government.

NEWSPAPERS AND MAGAZINES

Thousands of newspapers are printed every day all over the world. They are in many different languages. They help people learn about what's going on in the world.

Magazines usually come out once a week or once a month. Magazines often focus on a subject such as sports or news.

It's a Fact!

On a radio program broadcast in 1938, actors dramatized a story in which the Earth was attacked by aliens. Thousands of people thought the program was a real news story and panicked.

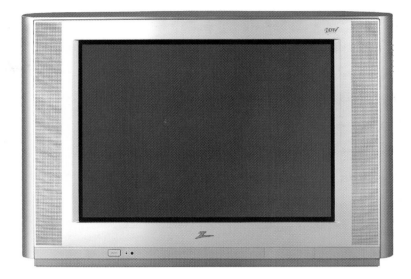

TELEVISION

Television lets billions of people across the world watch something at the very same time. There are many kinds of TV shows. Some, such as news shows, are shown live. Others are recorded on film and then shown later.

News shows are created by more than just the reporters you see on TV. A whole team helps to make the show.

More to Explore

Language

91

Measurement

Measurement is a way of showing the size, weight, or amount of something. Today, there are two main systems of measurement. One is a system that began in ancient times. The other is called the metric system. This newer system is used by scientists all over the world.

Some tools measure how long something is. Yardsticks and rulers measure this. They use inches, feet, and yards to measure.

Some tools measure something's weight. A scale does this. The ounce and the pound are used to measure weight.

Try This
Measure like an ancient Egyptian! Use the cubit. That's the distance between your elbow and the tip of your middle finger. How many cubits across is your desk? Then use the hand. That's the space it takes to lay down four fingers. How many hands wide is this book?

THE HISTORY OF MEASURING

Long ago, people usually used their bodies to measure things. For example, one unit of measurement was the length of a person's forearm. This system had problems, though. Since everyone's body is different, measurements were not the same each time. That's why people made up a way to measure that is always the same. We use a measurement system like that today.

Some measuring tools show how much of something there is. Measuring spoons and cups do this. They use measurements such as tablespoon, cup, pint, and quart.

Measurement is important in cooking and baking.

THE METRIC SYSTEM

The metric system began long ago in France. Units of measurement are based on the number 10. That makes things easy to figure out. Instead of feet, it uses *meters* to measure length. Instead of gallons, it uses *liters.* And instead of ounces, it uses *grams.*

Metal

Metals are solid materials that are found in the Earth's crust. All metals can be pounded into thin sheets. They can also be pulled or stretched to make wires and other shapes. When metals are polished, they become shiny. Metals have been used for thousands of years to make tools, jewelry, machines, and other objects.

It's a Fact!
There is more aluminum on Earth than any other metal.

Steel is the most useful metal. It does not cost a lot of money. It is strong and can be made into many shapes. Steel is not found in the Earth's crust. It is an *alloy.* Alloys are combinations of metals. Steel is made from iron, carbon, and other metals. The metals are heated in huge furnaces until they melt and combine to make steel.

Most metals are dug from the Earth's crust. Some are found close to the surface. Others are far below the surface. People and machines dig tunnels into the Earth to find rocks that contain metals. These rocks are called *ore.* The metal has to be taken out of the ore before it can be used.

It's a Fact!
The silver coins that are made today are not really silver. They are an alloy made by combining copper and nickel.

More to Explore

Earth

Money

Money is used to make trades. You exchange money when you buy something or pay for a service. Money can be cash. Cash is coins or paper money. Each country issues its own money. Money can also be other things that stand for cash, such as checks, credit cards, and debit cards.

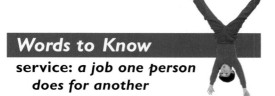

Words to Know
service: *a job one person does for another*

The first coins were probably made thousands of years ago. The coins were made of gold and silver. Paper money came a little later.

Most people keep their money in a bank. A bank is a business that keeps and lends money. The bank keeps records about the money each person puts into or takes out of the bank. Many people use special machines to get money out of their bank.

It's a Fact!
People have been saving money for thousands of years. Piggy banks from hundreds of years ago have been found. The first piggy banks were made of clay. They had to be cracked open to get the money out.

WHY WE USE MONEY

Long ago, people did not use money. They traded goods and services. For example, one person might have eggs. Another person might have wool. The two would trade those. But that system didn't always work. So, the idea of using money—a set value that could be used to pay for things—came about.

More to Explore
Business • Machines

Mountains

Mountains are rocky places that are higher than the land around them. Mountains are formed by the heat and pressure from melted rocks inside the Earth. The pressure pushes against the Earth's surface, or crust, and makes a mountain.

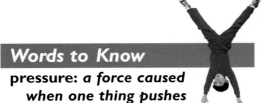

Words to Know

pressure: *a force caused when one thing pushes against another*

The higher you go on a mountain, the colder it gets. That is why it is always cooler at the top of a mountain than at the bottom. Some mountains are so high that they are covered with snow all year long.

Mount Shasta in California used to be a volcano.

There are many sports you can do on mountains. Skiing is one fun way to slide down a mountain. Snowboarding is also popular.

More to Explore

Earth • Rocks • Weather

MAKING MOUNTAINS

There are different types of mountains. Some mountains are made when part of the Earth's surface slips along a crack in the crust. The movement pushes the land up on one side of the crack and makes mountains. The Sierra Nevada mountains were formed this way.

Other mountains are formed by pressure inside the Earth. The pressure pushes the crust up and makes huge folds in the land. The folds are mountains.

A volcano happens when hot melted rock, called *lava,* bursts out of a crack in the Earth. The lava piles up and makes a mountain. When the lava cools, it becomes a rock.

The Sierra Nevadas

Mountains are always changing. Some mountains are still growing very slowly as pressure inside the Earth pushes against the Earth's crust. Other mountains are getting smaller. Wind, ice, and water wear away the rock. This is called *erosion* (i-RO-zhuhn).

Music

Music is a combination of sounds. There are all different kinds of music. People can sing music. Some is played on instruments, such as drums or the piano. If you play an instrument, you might like making your own music! A person who makes music is called a musician.

Words to Know

concert: *a musical performance*
orchestra: *a group of musicians who play certain instruments*
vibration: *a tiny movement back and forth that lasts for a while*

An orchestra is a group of musicians playing together. Orchestras usually play classical music. There are different groups of instruments in an orchestra. The person who leads an orchestra is called a *conductor.*

Music is written in a special language called *notes.* Musicians learn to read the language and play the music.

There are lots of different groups of people on the planet. Each group makes its own kind of music.

MUSICAL INSTRUMENTS

Musical instruments can be grouped by the way they make sounds.

String instruments are played by moving the strings and causing a vibration. Some string instruments are violins and guitars.

Wind instruments are played by the vibration of air through a tube. Flutes and saxophones are wind instruments.

Brass instruments make sounds when you blow into them. Trumpets and French horns are brass instruments.

Percussion (puhr-KUH-shuhn) instruments make music when you hit or shake them. Drums and cymbals are percussion instruments.

Pianos are actually percussion instruments with strings! When you hit a piano key, it causes a little hammer to hit a string inside the piano.

Many singers and musicians record their music. Then people can hear their music on the radio. Or they can buy a recording on a tape or CD.

More to Explore

Sound

North America

North America is the third-largest continent. The United States, Canada, and Mexico are all part of North America. The countries of Panama and Costa Rica are in North America, too. They are in a part called Central America. Central America has many countries.

The Rocky Mountains stretch across the continent. They run from Canada to Mexico.

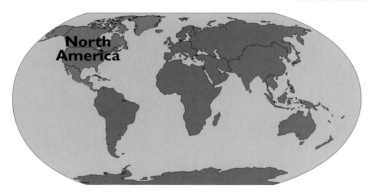

THE LAND

North America has all kinds of land. At one end, in Canada and Alaska, it is cold and icy. This part of the continent has lots of mountains. On the other end of the continent are steamy rain forests. Mexico has lots of areas like this. The land in the middle of the continent gets both hot and cold weather.

The Yucatan, Mexico

The middle part of North America is good for farming. The land there is usually flat, and the weather is good for growing crops.

The people of North America all look very different. There are lots of types of people who live there.

THE PEOPLE

People from all over the world have come to North America to live. The first people probably came to North America from the continent of Asia. These people formed several groups. One group in Mexico was called the Mayans (MY-uhns). These people built cities and pyramids out of stone.

Thousands of years later, people from Europe came to North America, too. North America gets parts of its culture from Europe. Even later, people also came to North America from Africa.

Many people have moved to North America from other lands. These people are called *immigrants* (I-mi-gruhnts). Many immigrants used to come to North America by boat.

It's a Fact!
• Canada is the world's second-largest country in size.
• The capital of Mexico is Mexico City. Millions of people live in that big city.

More to Explore

Africa • Asia • Europe • Language • Mammals • Mountains

North American Indians

North American Indians were the first groups of people to live in what is now the continent of North America. Different groups of Indians still live all over the United States and Canada. Each group has different languages and customs, or ways of doing things. They all have ideas and beliefs that are important to them. At the center of many of these beliefs is a deep respect and love for the Earth.

Sitting Bull was a great leader for his people, a group of American Indians called the Sioux. He fought to be sure they had land to hunt and live on.

North American Indians still live today in many parts of the United States and Canada. Many groups still celebrate special days in traditional ways.

LEGENDS

A legend is a story that has been passed down through many years. Parents told a story to their kids. When those children grew up, they told the story to their kids and so on. North American Indians have many legends. Some legends explain things that happen in the world, such as why the sun sets. Many stories have animals in them. Raven and Coyote are two popular characters. In the stories, these animals like to play tricks.

HOW THEY LIVED

Each North American Indian group used the things near them to live. They hunted animals for food and also ate plants that grew near their homes.

They also used materials they found in the area to build their shelters. North American Indians had lots of different types of homes. Some groups of Indians made houses out of wooden poles and animal skins. These homes looked a lot like tents. Other groups of American Indians built big, long buildings out of wood for their homes. Some groups even made houses out of a special clay that dried very hard.

A pueblo (PWAY-blo) house is made of a special clay. It is good for hot, dry places.

Some groups that often moved lived in houses made of animal skins. They could take these down easily when they needed to move.

Some groups built longhouses made of wood. Many families lived together inside the big buildings.

It's a Fact!

• November is National American Indian Heritage Month.

• The words *pecan, raccoon, woodchuck,* and *squash* all come from a North American Indian language.

More to Explore

Homes • Language • North America

Ocean

The ocean is a huge body of water that covers most of the Earth. It is separated into four smaller oceans by large pieces of land called continents. The four oceans are the Pacific Ocean, Atlantic Ocean, Arctic Ocean, and Indian Ocean. The water in the oceans is salty, so people and animals cannot drink it.

At certain times of the day, the waters of the ocean get higher near the shore. At other times, they get lower. These changes are called *tides*. When the tide is low, the water moves away from the shore. But some water stays in pools in the rocks. These pools are called *tide pools*. Many plants and animals live in tide pools.

Huge forests of seaweed grow on parts of the ocean floor. These forests are home to many ocean animals. Small animals hide in the seaweed. Larger animals come into the seaweed forests to find something to eat.

The place where the land and ocean meet is called the *shore*. Shores can be rocky, sandy, or marshy.

PARTS OF THE OCEAN

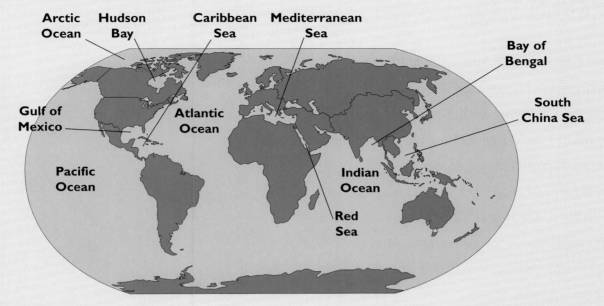

Arctic Ocean · Hudson Bay · Caribbean Sea · Mediterranean Sea · Bay of Bengal · South China Sea · Gulf of Mexico · Atlantic Ocean · Indian Ocean · Red Sea · Pacific Ocean

Smaller bodies of water in the ocean have different names.

A *sea* is smaller than an ocean and is partly or completely surrounded by land.

A *gulf* is part of an ocean that goes into the land.

A *bay* is like a gulf, but it is smaller.

The water in the ocean is always moving. Wind blowing across the water causes waves. The stronger the wind, the higher the waves. The waves crash down on the land.

The wind also causes *ocean currents.* These currents are like large rivers of water that move through the rest of the ocean.

More to Explore

Earth • Water • Weather

Pets

Pets are animals that people live with and take care of. People have been living with pets for thousands of years. The first pets were probably dogs. People who lived long ago taught wild dogs to help them hunt. Cats were pets thousands of years ago, too. Dogs and cats are still the most common pets.

Pets need people to take care of them. A pet must have food and water. It must also have places to live, sleep, and exercise. Many pets also need lots of love and attention to keep them happy.

ALL KINDS OF PETS

Pets are more than just cats and dogs. Lots of other animals can be pets, including rabbits, fish, gerbils, and horses. Some people even keep spiders as pets!

More to Explore

Fish • Jobs • Mammals • Spiders

It's a Fact!

Dogs can hear sounds that you can't. A dog whistle makes a very high sound. People cannot hear the sound, but dogs can.

You need to be sure that your pet stays healthy. If a pet gets sick, you can take it to a special animal doctor called a *veterinarian* (vet-uh-ruh-NAR-ee-uhn).

Some special pets are trained to help their owners. Guide dogs help lead blind people, for example.

TRAINED PETS

Many pets can be trained to do things:

• A dog can be trained to come when you call its name. It can also be trained to do tricks such as begging and rolling over.

• A cat can be trained to use a special box called a *litter box* when it has to go to the bathroom.

• A horse can be trained to let people ride on its back.

• Some birds can be trained to say words.

> ### It's a Fact!
> Chimpanzees can be trained to help people who are in wheelchairs. They bring things to the person. They can even be trained to pick up a ringing phone!

Plants

Plants grow everywhere except where it is cold all the time. Without plants, there would be no life on Earth. Plants give off the oxygen people and animals need to breathe. Plants also take harmful gases out of the air. Most of the food we eat comes from plants. Plants also give us materials to make things such as paper, cloth, medicine, and more.

Words to Know

nutrients: *things that help plants and animals live and grow*

Some people like to plant flowers in their yard. They enjoy the bright colors and sweet smells of the flowers.

The fruit of a plant is the part that holds the seeds. Some fruits, such as the dandelion, have seeds on the outside. Some fruits, such as the apple, have seeds on the inside.

Plants can't run away and hide, and they can't call for help. However, they have other ways to protect themselves. A cactus, for example, has sharp points that keep animals away!

THE PARTS OF A PLANT

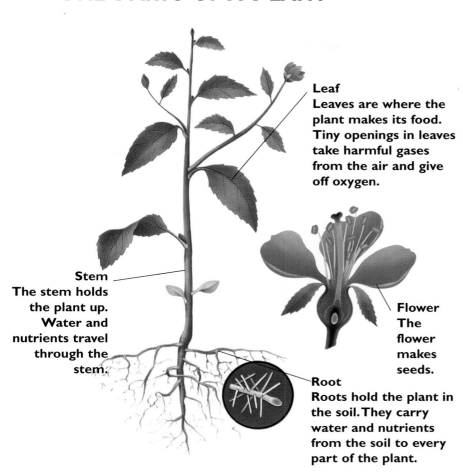

Leaf
Leaves are where the plant makes its food. Tiny openings in leaves take harmful gases from the air and give off oxygen.

Stem
The stem holds the plant up. Water and nutrients travel through the stem.

Flower
The flower makes seeds.

Root
Roots hold the plant in the soil. They carry water and nutrients from the soil to every part of the plant.

The plants in a garden grow food for the gardener to enjoy! These tomatoes are growing well in this garden.

PLANTS AND ANIMALS

Plants are living things. Like all living things, they need food and water. However, plants are different from humans and other animals in some important ways.

PLANTS

Make food from sunshine.
Cannot move from place to place.
Do not have good senses.

ANIMALS

Hunt, find, or grow food.
Move from place to place.
Have senses for smelling, feeling, hearing, seeing, and tasting.

More to Explore

Soil • Trees

Plastic

Plastic is not something that is found naturally on Earth. It has to be made by mixing chemicals. Plastic is important because it can be used in so many ways. It can be made into almost any shape. It can be hard or soft, clear or brightly colored, stiff or bendable.

Plastic can be made in all different colors. The hot plastic is poured into a mold, where it will harden.

Words to Know

artificial: *not real*
chemicals: *materials that cause changes when added to other materials*
mold: *to shape*

It's a Fact!

• Some plastics are stronger than metal—even steel!

• One problem with plastic is it takes a long time to *decay,* or fall apart. It is important to recycle plastics so they can be used again. Otherwise, they will fill up the dumps and landfills.

THE USES OF PLASTIC

Today, plastic is used in everything from toys and radios to artificial hips and cars! Plastics are important because they can be used in ways that other materials cannot.

Plastics are lighter than metal, but they can be just as strong. Plastic is also lighter than glass, and it does not break easily. It can be used for windows, eyeglasses, and food containers.

More to Explore

Inventions • Metal • Trash and Recycling

Postal Service

The postal system allows people to send and get letters and packages. Postal workers pick up, sort, and deliver mail. You can send mail through the post office to everyone from your next-door neighbor to someone in another part of the world. It usually takes just a few days for the mail to get there.

STAMPS

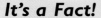

Stamps show that you have paid to have a piece of mail sent. Post offices all over the world sell stamps. Many people also like to collect stamps.

George Washington was on one of the first stamps in the United States. He was honored because he was the first president of the United States.

THE HISTORY OF THE POST

Mail has been around a long time! People have been sending and getting letters for hundreds of years. Before the telephone was invented, this is how people stayed in touch.

Not everyone long ago could send letters, though. Many people did not know how to read and write. And if they did, it cost a lot of money to send a letter. Few people had enough money to do it.

Helen Byrt
1234 Good St.
Chicago, IL
60626

111

HOW MAIL IS SENT

1. Letters and packages are put in a mailbox.

2. Post office workers pick up the mail.

3. The mail is sorted according to where it is going.

4. The mail travels by truck, train, or plane.

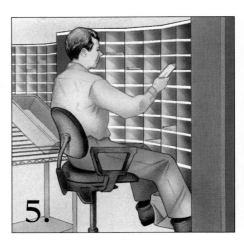

5. The mail is sorted again.

6. A mail carrier delivers the mail.

It's a Fact!
Letters today are often sorted by machines. These machines can sort about 36,000 letters per hour!

More to Explore

Jobs • Telephone

Religion

A religion is a set of beliefs. There are many different religions around the world. Each religion has different beliefs. People honor their god or gods in religion. They usually do this by meeting together and worshiping. The world's main religions are Buddhism, Christianity, Hinduism, Islam, Judaism, and Sikhism.

Christians worship in a building called a *church.*

Buddhists usually pray to a statue of Buddha such as this one.

BUDDHISM

Buddhists believe in the teachings of a man named Buddha. Buddha lived long ago. He taught people how to find *enlightenment,* or an understanding of the world. Buddhists believe the way we think and act is more important than the things we own. One Buddhist holy day is Vesak, which is also called Buddha Day. This day celebrates the birth and death of Buddha.

The cross is a symbol of Christianity.

CHRISTIANITY

The Christian faith is based on the teachings of Jesus Christ. Christians believe that Christ is the son of God. They believe that Christ died to save believers from sin. Christian holy days include Christmas, which is the day Christ was born, and Easter, which is when Christ rose from the dead.

113

SIKHISM

The Sikh religion teaches that God is found in all things. A man named Guru Nanak began teaching this faith a long time ago. Sikhs worship so they can form a close relationship with God. Sikhs celebrate the birthday of Guru Nanak, as well as Baisakhi, which is the New Year.

Sikhs worship in a building called a *gurdwara.*

ISLAM

People who follow Islam are called *Muslims.* Muslims promise to obey the will of Allah, or God. They believe a man named Muhammad brought messages from Allah. Islamic festivals include Id al-Fitr, which is the end of Ramadan. Ramadan is a sacred monthlong holiday. It is a time for thinking about others.

Muslims pray many times a day. They point in the direction of Mecca when they pray. Mecca is a holy city to Muslims.

HINDUISM

Hindus worship the gods Brahma, Vishnu, and Shiva, along with other gods and goddesses. Hindus believe that they will be born again to another life. Hindu holy days include Divali, a New Year's festival of lights, and Holi, a spring festival.

The Hindu god Shiva has four hands. Each hand stands for something. One hand holds a drum that stands for creation. Another hand holds a small flame that stands for destruction. The other two hands show protection and teaching. Shiva is a very powerful god.

The Star of David is a symbol of Judaism. The six points on the star show God's power in all six directions: north, south, east, west, up, and down.

Jews have ceremonies for certain holidays. Jews have a seder (SAY-duhr) to celebrate the holiday of Passover. During seder, they tell stories and eat special foods.

JUDAISM

People who follow Judaism are called Jews. Jews believe that they are God's chosen people. Jewish holy days include Yom Kippur, a serious day of fasting (not eating) and praying, and Passover, a celebration of when Jews were released from slavery in Egypt.

More to Explore

Holidays

115

Reptiles

Reptiles are animals that have thick, dry skin covered with scales. Except for snakes, reptiles have four legs and claws that they use for walking, digging, and climbing. Reptiles lay eggs that are covered with tough shells. Snakes, lizards, turtles, alligators, and crocodiles are all reptiles.

Turtles come in all shapes and sizes. Some little turtles like to live in lakes and ponds. Other huge turtles live in the ocean.

It's a Fact!
Turtles and tortoises are different. Tortoises only live on land. They are found in dry places. Turtles spend time in the water and on land.

Snakes and some lizards keep growing as long as they live. Their skin doesn't grow along with them, though. So these reptiles shed their skin when it gets too small. Snakes shed their skin in one long piece. The skin that is left behind looks like a hollow snake!

STAYING WARM
All reptiles are cold-blooded. That means the temperature of their blood is always the same as the temperature of the air around them. Reptiles like to lie in the sun to get warm. When it is cold, reptiles don't move around much.

An iguana keeps warm in the sun.

CROCODILES AND ALLIGATORS

Crocodiles and alligators are both long reptiles with big teeth. They both also spend a lot of time in the water. However, they are different in some ways.

AN ALLIGATOR HAS...
A wide, rounded snout.
Large front teeth that fit into pits in the upper jaw and cannot be seen when the mouth is closed.

A CROCODILE HAS...
A pointed snout.
Large front teeth that fit into notches in the upper jaw and are quite visible.

The Parson's chameleon can change the color of its skin to match the land around it. This is called *camouflage.* Some reptiles use camouflage to hide. It can help keep them safe from their enemies.

It's a Fact!

• The world's largest lizard is the Komodo dragon. It can be 10 feet long and weigh 300 pounds.

• The African black mamba is the fastest snake in the world. It can move seven miles per hour. That's faster than most people can run!

Reticulated python

More to Explore

Ocean

117

Rescue

Sometimes people need help. Someone may be hurt, or someone may be in danger. That's when you need the help of a rescue worker! People may need an ambulance, a firefighter, or a police officer. In many places, you can dial 9-1-1 on a phone, and help will be on the way!

It's a Fact!
Never call 9-1-1 as a joke! You can get into trouble. Your prank call could keep someone who really needs help from getting it in time.

POLICE
Police officers help fight crime. They remind people to follow the laws. If someone breaks the law, the police officers may arrest the person and put him or her in jail. Police officers drive cars that have special radios. The radios are used to tell police officers where help is needed. Some police officers have dogs that are specially trained to help with police work.

GETTING HELP
If someone is hurt or sick and needs emergency help, here is how you can help:
- Dial 9-1-1.
- Don't hang up. It may take a few rings. You may get a recording that tells you to hold on.
- Tell the person where you are.
- Stay calm. Speak slowly, and tell why you need help.
- Follow the instructions the person on the phone gives you.

EMERGENCY - CALL 9-1-1

FIREFIGHTERS

Firefighters arrive on the scene of a fire in a fire truck. A fire engine carries big, long hoses to spray water on a fire. Firefighters have axes and other equipment in the truck. Some fire trucks also have a ladder that can go up high to rescue people from the windows of a burning building.

Pumping truck

Aerial ladder truck

Elevating platform truck

AMBULANCE

An ambulance is a vehicle that takes people to get medical help. An ambulance can pick someone up and take them to the hospital. It also has all kinds of equipment to help people. The people who drive the ambulance are trained to help.

More to Explore

Cars • Jobs

Rivers and Streams

Rivers are water that flows from higher ground to lower ground. Rivers keep flowing until they join with another river or until they reach the ocean. Streams are like rivers, but they are smaller.

Streams often begin in mountains. Sometimes the stream water is melted snow from the mountaintop.

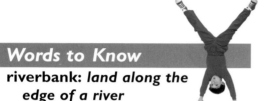

The Mississippi River is very long. It runs from the top of the United States to the bottom.

RIVER AND STREAM ANIMALS

Many animals live in or beside rivers or streams. Animals like fish, crocodiles, ducks, and beaver spend most of their time in the water. Turtles, snakes, frogs, and otters often live along riverbanks.

More to Explore

Mountain • Ocean • Water

120

Rocks

Rocks are found everywhere. Mountains are formed by rocks that are higher than the land around them. There are rocks under the ocean, too. Even the soil is made of tiny pieces of rock. There are three kinds of rock. Each is formed in a different way.

Lava is hot, melted rock.

IGNEOUS ROCK

Inside the Earth there is hot, liquid rock called *magma*. Sometimes magma is forced up to the surface and flows out of cracks or volcanoes. When this happens, the liquid rock is called *lava*. The lava cools and becomes hard rock.

SEDIMENTARY ROCK

Wind, rain, and water wear rock down into tiny pieces called *sediment* (SE-duh-muhnt). The sediment is carried away by water until it settles on the ground or at the bottom of a river. Bits of dead plants and animals settle there, too. Layer after layer of sediment piles up. The weight of the top layers presses down and cements the bottom layers together. They become sedimentary rock.

METAMORPHIC ROCK

Metamorphic (me-tuh-MOR-fik) rock starts as igneous or sedimentary rock deep in the Earth, where it is very hot. The heat makes the rock soft. Then pressure inside the Earth squeezes the rock and makes it change. When the rock cools, it gets hard again, but it looks different than before.

More to Explore

Earth • Soil

Science

Science is the study of the world. People who work in science are called scientists. *Scientists observe what happens. They collect facts and organize them to show how things go together. They work to figure out how things happen and why they happen. Then they often use that information to make changes in the world.*

Words to Know
fact: something that is always true

Scientists have many tools that help them learn more about the world. Some tools make faraway things look closer. Scientists use tools called *telescopes* to look far away in space.

DISCOVERIES AND INVENTIONS

A discovery is learning about something that has always been true. A discovery takes place when someone observes things happening and figures out why they happen.

An invention is an object or idea that someone creates. It did not exist until it was invented. Scientists use discoveries about the world when they invent.

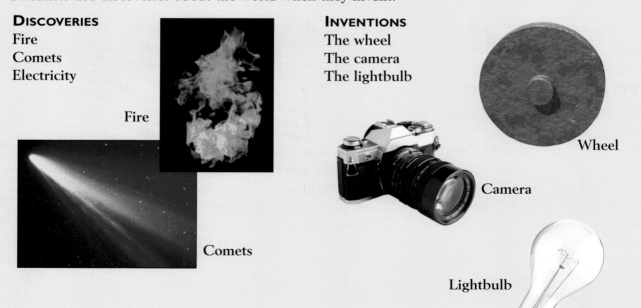

DISCOVERIES
Fire
Comets
Electricity

Fire

Comets

INVENTIONS
The wheel
The camera
The lightbulb

Wheel

Camera

Lightbulb

Some scientists use tools that help them see very small things. With microscopes such as this one, people can study things that are too tiny to be seen with the eyes alone.

TYPES OF SCIENCE

There are many different kinds of science. Each kind has its own name. People who work in different sciences observe and study different things.

SCIENCE	WHAT SCIENTISTS STUDY
astronomy	space
botany	plants
chemistry	what things are made of and what happens when they combine
geology	rocks, fossils
meteorology	weather
physics	energy and force
zoology	animals

THE SCIENTIFIC METHOD

Scientists look at the world and try to figure out how things work. They think of new ways to use what they know. Then they test those ideas. Most scientists follow certain steps to do this. These steps are called the *scientific method.*

Step 1: Come up with a question to be answered or a problem to be solved.

Step 2: Collect information about the problem or question.

Step 3: Make a guess about the answer to the question or solution to the problem.

Step 4: Do experiments to test the guess.

Step 5: Use what is learned to answer the question or solve the problem.

It's a Fact!

One of the first discoveries ever made was how to make fire. No one knows who actually made this important discovery, or how. Perhaps someone accidentally made a spark by banging two rocks together.

More to Explore

Electricity • Inventions • Jobs

The Seasons

Seasons are changes in the weather that happen during the year. There are four seasons: spring, summer, autumn or fall, and winter. The seasons happen because the Earth leans as it travels around the sun. That means that at certain times, more sunlight reaches some parts of the Earth than others. The places that get more sunlight are warmer.

Leaves on the ground are one sign that fall is here.

THE WEATHER OF THE SEASONS

Each season has its own kind of weather.

SPRING
In the spring, the weather gets warmer. There is often a lot of rain. Plants and trees start to grow.

SUMMER
In the summer, it can be very hot. The days are long, and the nights are short.

WINTER
In the winter, it is cold. In many parts of the world, the weather is snowy. The days are short, and the nights are long.

AUTUMN
In the autumn, the weather gets cooler. Most plants stop growing. Many trees lose their leaves.

WHY SEASONS CHANGE

It takes the Earth one year to revolve around the sun. As the Earth revolves, different parts get more sunshine. The seasons change, too.

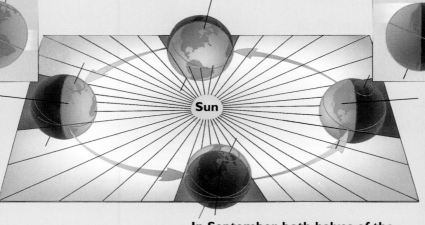

In March, both halves of the Earth get almost the same amount of sunlight. It is spring in the top half. It is autumn in the bottom half.

In June, the top half of the Earth gets a lot of sunlight. It is summer there. The bottom half gets less sunlight. It is winter there.

Sun

In December, the bottom half of the Earth gets a lot of sunlight. It is summer there. The top half gets less sunlight. It is winter there.

In September, both halves of the Earth get almost the same amount of sunlight. It is autumn in the top half. It is spring in the bottom half.

Words to Know

temperature: *how hot or cold something is*

Trees can tell us a lot about the seasons. In the spring, some trees grow green leaves. In the summer, trees are bright green. In the fall, some leaves turn orange and fall off. In the winter, many trees have no leaves.

More to Explore

Earth • Trees • Weather

125

The Senses

Your senses tell you about the world around you. You have five senses: sight, hearing, touch, smell, and taste. Different parts of your body collect information for each sense and send it to your brain. Then your brain tells you what the information means and what to do about it.

All of our senses are important! We use each of our senses every day.

HOW YOU USE YOUR SENSES

Different parts of your body collect information for each sense. These parts are called the *sense organs.*

SENSE	SENSE ORGAN
Sight	Eyes
Hearing	Ears
Smell	Nose
Taste	Tongue
Touch	Skin

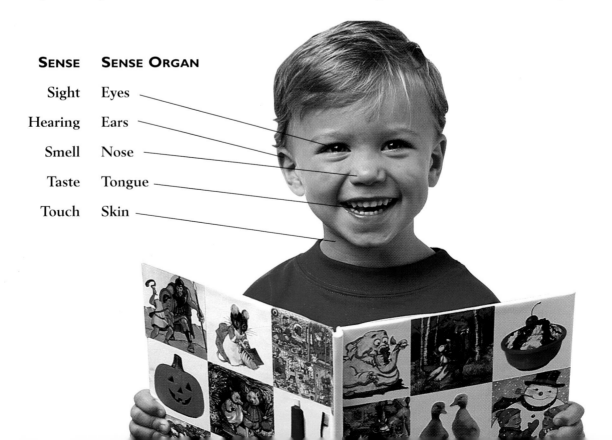

THE EAR

Your ears let you hear. The outer ear acts like a funnel. It collects sounds and sends them inside the ear, where they bump into the eardrum. The sounds make the eardrum move back and forth, or *vibrate.* The sounds travel to the inner ear. Here they change into signals that go to the brain. When the signals reach the brain, you hear the sounds.

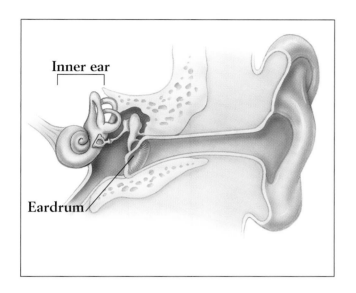

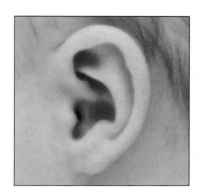

THE EYE

Your eyes let you see color, size, and shapes. Light enters your eye through a dark opening in the middle called the *pupil.* The light travels to the back of the eye where there is a lining called the *retina.* The retina sends messages to your brain about what you are seeing.

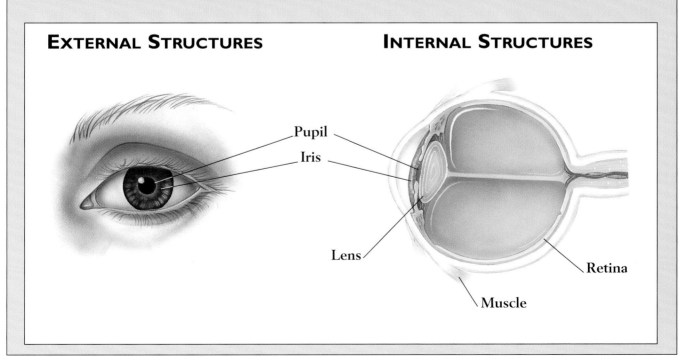

EXTERNAL STRUCTURES

INTERNAL STRUCTURES

Pupil

Iris

Lens

Retina

Muscle

It's a Fact!

• The tiny hairs in your nose are important. They trap tiny bits of dirt and dust and keep them from getting inside your body.

• Did you know your senses of taste and smell work together? Your brain receives messages from the tongue and nose to give you your sense of taste. That's why food sometimes  tastes different when you have a cold and your nose is plugged up!

THE NOSE

Your nose lets you smell things. Tiny parts in the air called *molecules* have smells. When you breathe, some of these molecules go through your nostrils. Special cells in the top part of your nose get messages from these molecules. They send the messages to your brain.

THE SKIN

Skin gives you your sense of touch. Your whole body is covered with skin, so you use this sense all the time. There are thousands of tiny nerve endings in your skin. When something touches these nerve endings, they send messages to the brain. The brain tells the rest of the body what to do. That's why you pull away from something that is hot or sharp without even thinking about it!

THE TONGUE

Your tongue lets you taste things. It is covered with thousands of tiny cells called *taste buds.* The taste buds send messages to the brain. Different parts of your tongue tell about different tastes:

You taste salty foods here.

You taste bitter foods here.

You taste sour foods here and here.

You taste sweet foods here.

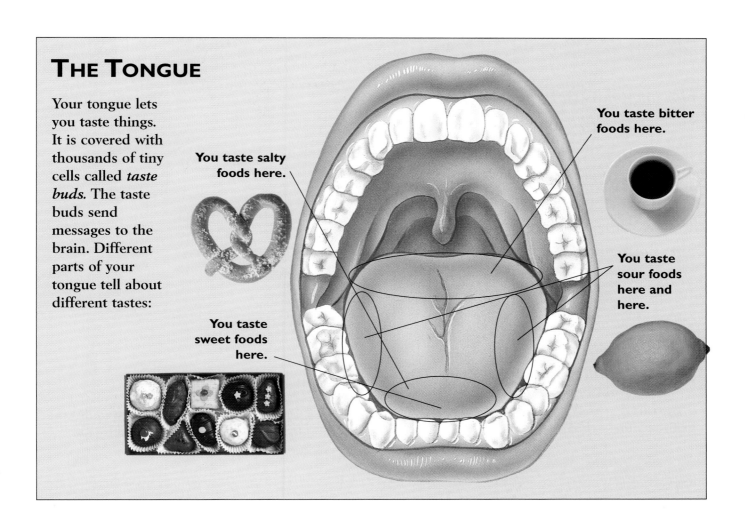

It's a Fact!

Your ears are important for more than hearing. They also give you your sense of balance. A liquid in the middle ear tells your brain when your head moves. Your brain then signals the rest of the body so you don't lose your balance.

Words to Know

cells: *tiny parts that make up all living things*

More to Explore

The Body • Colors • Health • Light • Sound

Ships and Boats

Ships and boats carry people and goods across water. If you have ridden on a ferry, a sailboat, a rowboat, or even a jet ski, you're a boater! There are many kinds of ships and boats. Ships and boats are alike, except for the size. Ships are larger than boats. Some boats do special jobs. Others are just for fun.

Words to Know

cargo: *things that are being moved from one place to another*
goods: *things that are sold*

A submarine is a boat that can go under the water. Submarines are often used by the military.

It's a Fact!

• About 95 percent of all the things sold in the world are moved from one place to another by a ship.

• In 1912, the ship *Titanic* hit an iceberg and sank. About 1,500 people died in this famous shipwreck.

The tugboat does just what its name says—it can tug, or *tow,* a big ship. The tugboat has the important job of guiding big ships in and out of shallow and narrow areas.

Some people even *live* on boats! China is a country with lots of rivers. Some people there live on boats. An entire family may live on a boat just like this one, which is called a *sampan.*

Boats and ships have been important to help people move around. Long ago, ships were the only way for people to cross the oceans. In 1620, people sailed from Europe to North America on the *Mayflower.* They made America their new home.

Some types of boats are very small. This kayak is only big enough for one person.

A sailboat uses wind power to move. The wind catches the fabric in the sail and pushes the boat along. The rudder on the bottom helps to steer the boat.

THE PARTS OF A BIG SHIP

There are many different kinds of big ships, but most have the same basic parts. A container ship carries large amounts of cargo across the sea.

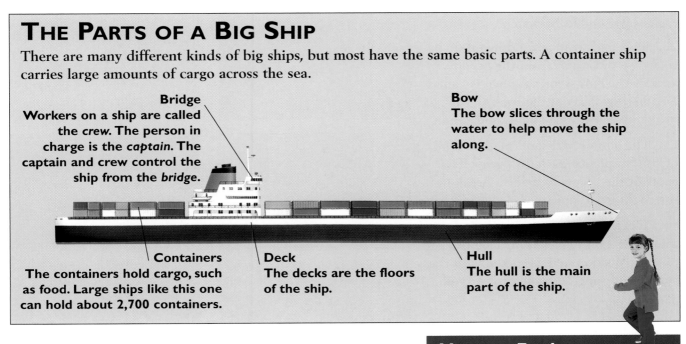

Bridge
Workers on a ship are called the *crew.* The person in charge is the *captain.* The captain and crew control the ship from the *bridge.*

Bow
The bow slices through the water to help move the ship along.

Containers
The containers hold cargo, such as food. Large ships like this one can hold about 2,700 containers.

Deck
The decks are the floors of the ship.

Hull
The hull is the main part of the ship.

More to Explore

Europe • North America • Rivers and Streams

Soil

Soil covers much of the Earth's surface. It is made up of a combination of things such as sand, clay, tiny pieces of rock, and bits of dead plants and animals. Soil also contains water, air, and minerals such as quartz. Worms, insects, and other small animals live in soil.

Some soil is good for growing plants. It is full of rotted plant and animal materials. This gives the soil a lot of nutrients. It looks very rich and dark.

WHERE SOIL IS FROM

1. Many millions of years ago, before the time of the dinosaurs, there was no soil on Earth. There were only large rocks surrounded by water.

2. Rain and wind wore down the rocks. So did water from the oceans and rivers. This wearing down is called *weathering.* Parts of the rock slowly broke up to become stones and sand.

3. The stones and sand made a kind of soil, so plants started to grow. The roots of the plants helped to break up the rocks even more.

4. When plants and animals died, they rotted on the ground. Tiny pieces of these dead materials mixed with the stones and sand to make dirt, or *soil.*

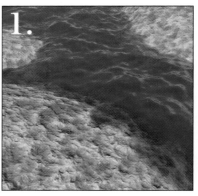

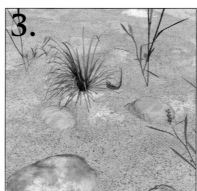

132

More to Explore

Earth • Plants • Rocks

Sound

Sound is made when objects move back and forth very quickly, or vibrate. The vibrations move away from the object in sound waves. When these waves reach your ear, you hear the sound. Sound can travel through air, water, wood, and even metal.

More to Explore

Music • The Senses

Music is just one type of sound. Some machines, such as stereos and headphones, help us hear music.

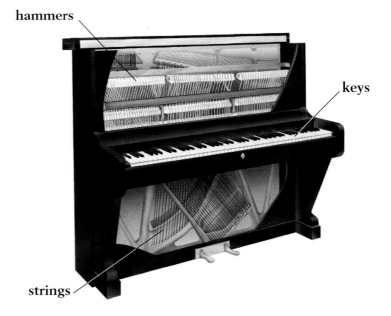

hammers

keys

strings

YOUR HEARING

Without your ears, you wouldn't hear sound. Sound goes into your outer ear and then to your middle ear. Inside the middle ear is a liquid and some tiny hairs. The sound travels through the liquid and makes the tiny hairs move. They send messages to your brain. Then your brain turns these messages into sounds that you understand.

Different objects make different sounds when they vibrate. Some sounds are more pleasant than others. The sounds of musical instruments are all created by vibrations. When you press a piano key, it makes a hammer hit a string inside the piano. The string vibrates and makes a sound.

South America

South America is the fourth-largest continent in the world. The world's longest mountain chain, the Andes, stretches through seven countries there. Much of the land in South America is rain forest. The people of South America are a blend of many cultures, including Portuguese, Spanish, African, and the native peoples.

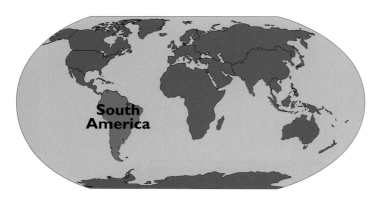

Angel Falls is the world's highest waterfall. It is in the country of Venezuela.

WILDLIFE

The rain forests, mountains, and coasts are home to many interesting plants and animals.

The jaguar is a big cat that lives in the rain forests of South America. It is known for its power and its spots.

More kinds of birds are found in South America than in any other continent. The harpy eagle lives in tropical forests.

Howler monkeys live in tropical areas, too. These monkeys howl to communicate. The howl can be heard for miles!

The Galapagos tortoise is a type of turtle that can get *very* big. It lives in islands in South America. A tortoise can sometimes live more than 100 years!

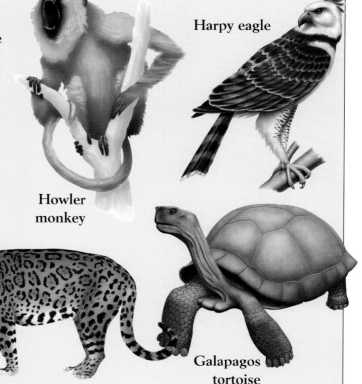

Harpy eagle

Howler monkey

Jaguar

Galapagos tortoise

Words to Know

coast: *land near the shore of a body of water*
continent: *a large body of land*
crop: *plants grown for food*
culture: *the way of life of a group of people*

The Andes

The Amazon rain forest

THE LAND

South America has beautiful land with lots of rain forests and mountains.

The Andes Mountains stand out in the landscape of South America. These mountains are the longest and one of the highest in the world. They run through most of the continent.

The Amazon rain forest is another important land feature in South America. This area is rich with plant and animal life. It is the biggest rain forest in the world!

THE PEOPLE

South America has a lot of different cultures. Some of the cultures come from Europe and Africa, and some of the cultures are from native peoples who have lived in the area for thousands of years.

Many native people of South America live in the mountains. They are in some of the highest places in the world. The mountain air is thin, but over time, the people adapted to this.

Most people in South America live in cities. Almost all of the people live close to the coast. Most people speak the Spanish language.

Coffee is an important crop in South America. It is grown in many places. Evergreen trees produce the coffee bean.

More to Explore

Africa • Birds • Europe • Forest • Language • Mountains • Plants • Trees

135

Space

Space is the world outside our Earth. Space goes on and on—farther than even the most powerful telescope can see. There are many objects in space. There are other planets. There are also moons, stars, comets, and meteors. There probably are things in space that no one even knows about yet.

A meteor is a piece of rock that enters the air around the Earth. Traveling through the air makes the rock so hot that it starts to burn. It looks like a star that is falling toward Earth. That's why people sometimes call meteors *shooting stars.*

Words to Know

astronaut: *a person who travels into space*

It's a Fact!

Space goes on and on. Even if you could travel as fast as light, you couldn't reach the end of space. Scientists don't even know where the end of space is!

DAY AND NIGHT

The planets all spin around in space. This is called *rotating.* The time it takes a planet to make one spin is one day on that planet. Earth takes about 24 hours to spin around once. So a day on Earth is 24 hours long. Other planets spin faster or slower than Earth. Jupiter is the slowest. One day on Jupiter is the same as almost ten years on Earth!

Rotating is also what makes day and night on the planets. The part of a planet that faces the sun has day. The part that is away from the sun has night. As the planet spins, day changes to night and then goes back to day.

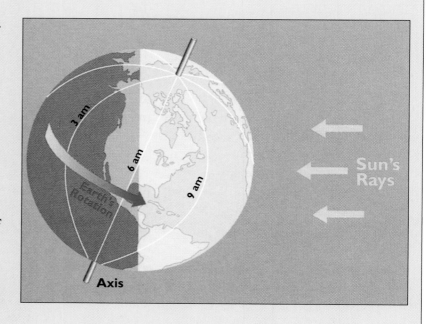

PLANETS

Earth is one of the nine planets that travel around the Sun. The planets are all different.

5. Jupiter

4. Mars

3. Earth

2. Venus

1. Mercury

9. Pluto

6. Saturn

7. Uranus

8. Neptune

1. Mercury is very hot and cold. It has no moon.

2. Venus has clouds around it. It has no moon.

3. Earth has water and land and breathable air. It is cool on the surface. Earth has one moon.

4. Mars is red and rocky and cold and dry. It has volcanoes and canyons. Mars has two moons.

5. Jupiter is the largest planet. It's mostly made of gases. Jupiter has 16 moons.

6. Saturn has rings around it. It has 18 moons.

7. Uranus is a blue-green color and mostly made of water. It has 15 moons.

8. Neptune is mostly made of water. It is very windy and has eight moons.

9. Pluto is the smallest planet. It is sometimes closer to the Sun than Neptune. It has one moon.

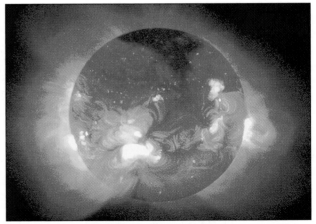

The Sun is 93 million miles away from Earth. Light from the Sun travels very fast. It takes a ray of sunlight just a little more than eight minutes to reach Earth!

Do you see pictures when you look up at the stars? People long ago did. They imagined that there were lines drawn between the stars to make pictures. They called these star pictures *constellations.* Each constellation has a name.

The Sun and the stars that you see in the night sky are all part of the Milky Way galaxy. A galaxy is a huge group of stars that move together in space. Earth and the other planets that travel around the Sun are all part of the Milky Way galaxy.

STARS

Stars are the brightest objects in space. The Sun is a star. It is not the brightest star. It only looks that way to us because it is closer to Earth than any other star.

Stars are made of hot gases. They are bright because the gases are burning. Every star is like a big ball of fire in space.

Try This

Go outside with an adult after dark and look up. Can you find the constellation called the Big Dipper?

People used to only dream about traveling in space. During the 20th century, that dream came true. Astronauts fly into space in an aircraft called a spaceship. There is no air in space. The astronauts have to wear special suits that gave them air to breathe while they explore outside the ship.

More to Explore

Aircraft • Earth • Explorers

Spiders

Spiders are animals that have eight legs and two body parts. Most spiders have eight eyes, but they do not have feelers. Spiders make a liquid called silk. When the silk comes out of openings called spinnerets, it hardens into threads. Spiders use these threads to make webs.

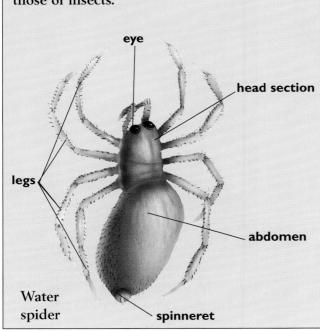

Some of the threads in a spiderweb are sticky and some are not. When an insect touches the web, the sticky threads grab it. As the insect tries to get free, the web moves and alerts the spider. The spider hurries down the nonsticky threads. It bites the insect and wraps it up in spider silk.

THE PARTS OF A SPIDER

The parts of a spider are a little different from those of insects.

eye

head section

legs

abdomen

Water spider

spinneret

All spiders use poison to kill their prey. However, only a few spiders have poison that could kill a person. The most poisonous spiders are the brown recluse, the black widow, and some tarantulas, such as this one.

More to Explore
Insects

Sports

Sports are games and contests in which people are moving and playing. In sports, people will often compete against others. Sometimes people play with other people on teams. The teams then play each other. In some sports, though, people play alone.

Soccer is a sport that is popular all around the world. In most countries, soccer is actually called *football!*

Words to Know

athlete: *a person who participates in a sport*
compete: *to try to win*

It's a Fact!
About 30 million men, women, and children play in soccer leagues.

THERE HAVE ALWAYS BEEN SPORTS!

Early people had to run, jump, and climb just to survive every day. Sports grew out of these activities. Some of the first organized sports were wrestling and boxing. Hunting and archery contests were also held long ago. And it is believed that the first ball game was played by Indians in Central America.

People of all ages like sports. Baseball is a popular game for kids to play.

WHY PEOPLE LIKE SPORTS

People play sports for many reasons. Some people play to keep healthy. Others just play for fun. Some people even play sports for their jobs! You might see these athletes on TV.

Some people don't like to play sports. They like to *watch* sports. Sports that people like to watch are called *spectator sports.* Soccer, football, basketball, and baseball are examples of spectator sports.

OLYMPIC GAMES

The Olympic Games gather the best athletes from all over the world to compete. The Olympics are held every two years in different countries. The Summer Olympics have events such as running, gymnastics, and water sports. The Winter Olympics have winter sports, such as skiing, sledding, and ice skating.

TEAM SPORTS AND INDIVIDUAL SPORTS

TEAM

baseball

basketball

football

hockey

soccer

INDIVIDUAL

archery

golf

running

swimming

tennis

More to Explore

Health

Telephone

A telephone is used to send sound or other information over a distance. Telephones help people communicate. There are different kinds of telephones, but each one has a part for speaking into and a part for listening.

There are millions of telephone lines all over the world. These lines help connect people so they can talk to each other.

Words to Know

invent: *to make for the first time*
operator: *a person who helps others make phone calls*

TELEPHONES LONG AGO AND TODAY

Telephones were invented more than 100 years ago by a man named Alexander Graham Bell. The first telephones did not have dials. Instead, people picked up the phone and talked to a person called an *operator.* The operator would connect the call.

Telephones today are different. Many homes have cordless phones. This type of phone is really a radio and telephone in one. Then there are cell phones, which let people make and receive calls from anywhere! Telephone lines can also be used to send information between computers. This is how the Internet works.

It's a Fact!

• The first words spoken on a phone were Alexander Graham Bell calling his assistant. He said something like, "Mr. Watson, come here. I want to see you."

• The first cell phone weighed two pounds.

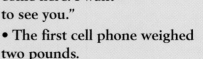

More to Explore

Inventions • Machines

Time

Time is how long it takes for something to happen. People use the movement of the Earth to measure time. They also use machines such as clocks and watches to help track time.

WHAT SOME TIME WORDS MEAN

There are certain special words that we use to measure time. These words are *second, minute, hour, day, month,* and *year.*

Has anyone ever told you that they'll be with you in "just a second"? That means they'll be with you quickly. A *second* is a very short period of time. There are 60 seconds in a *minute.* A minute is still pretty short. There are 60 minutes in an *hour.* An hour is about two TV shows long.

You need 24 hours to make up a *day.* And there are about 30 days in a *month.* December is an example of a month. There are 12 months in each *year.*

HOURS, MINUTES, AND SECONDS

Thousands of years ago, a group of people created a system of measuring time. We still use that system today. They decided an hour would be made up of 60 minutes. One minute would be made up of 60 seconds. They used the number 60 because it is easy to divide into smaller parts.

The way people have measured time has changed over the years. People used to use tools such as a sundial to keep track of time. A sundial used the sun and shadows to tell the time.

More to Explore

Earth • Machines • Measurement

143

Trains

Trains carry lots of different things. Some carry people, and some carry freight, or things to be moved. Trains that carry people are called passenger trains. Trains are a good method of transportation. They use less fuel than cars and trucks.

Trains today can move very fast. Some trains go more than 150 miles per hour!

TRAINS LONG AGO AND NOW

The first trains were wagons pulled on a track by people or by horses. Then the steam train was invented. Later, trains used diesel fuel. Today, many trains run on electricity.

More to Explore

Electricity • Inventions • Jobs • Machines

Some big cities have special trains. These trains help people move around the city easily. These trains sometimes run below ground.

144

It's a Fact!
The United States has about 149,000 miles of railroad tracks. That's enough to circle the Earth almost six times!

Railroads are usually laid as one long, connected track. But sometimes two lines of track come together. Switches are used to move trains onto different parts of the track. A movable section of track directs the train from one part to another.

KINDS OF FREIGHT CARS

Trains use different kinds of cars to carry freight. Each one is designed to make loading, carrying, and unloading different kinds of freight easier. For example, the boxcar can carry boxes inside it. The piggyback car can carry something large on top of it.

Boxcar

Piggyback car

The person who drives the train is called the *engineer.*

Words to Know

freight: *things that are being shipped from one place to another*
passenger: *person who is traveling*

145

Trash and Recycling

Trash is anything that people don't want and throw away. Another word for trash is garbage. In many parts of the world, workers collect trash and take it to a dump or landfill. However, some trash is recycled, or used again.

Landfills and dumps fill up quickly. There is not enough room for all the trash that people throw away. That is why recycling is so important.

Americans throw away more than 200 million tons of garbage each year. That's a lot of trash!

Words to Know

code: *mark that has a special meaning*

WHAT TO RECYCLE

Cities and towns have rules about what can be recycled. Many communities recycle things like:

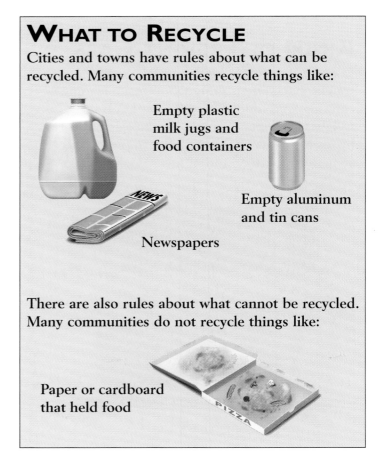

Empty plastic milk jugs and food containers

Empty aluminum and tin cans

Newspapers

There are also rules about what cannot be recycled. Many communities do not recycle things like:

Paper or cardboard that held food

TAKING CARE OF TRASH

Trash must be handled correctly. Otherwise, it can cause many problems.

• If trash gets into rivers, ponds, and lakes, it can pollute the water. It might make it unsafe to drink.

• Burning trash is not a good idea because the smoke can pollute the air. And smoke from some burning materials is dangerous to breathe.

• If trash gets thrown on the ground, it can attract insects and other animals that can spread disease.

Packaging foam can take more than 50 years to break down and become part of the earth. Too much foam in the garbage is a bad thing.

HOW TRASH IS RECYCLED

Trash can be recycled in many ways. Some things are recycled when someone else uses them. Many people recycle clothing by giving it to organizations that help others.

Other things are recycled by being used to make new products. For example, glass can be melted down and used to make new glass. Newspapers can be shredded and used to make new paper.

It's a Fact!
• When landfills run out of room for trash, they can be recycled, too. Workers put a thick layer of dirt over the landfill. Then they plant trees and other plants there. Some landfills end up as parks or golf courses!
• Recycling saves trees. It takes thousands of trees to make the paper to print one day's news in a large city.

WHAT TO RECYCLE

Different kinds of plastic are recycled in different ways. In the United States, plastics that can be recycled are marked with a code. The code is a triangle with a number inside it. The number tells what kind of plastic the object is made from. That way the recycling company knows what to do with the plastic.

It is important to know what kinds of plastic can be recycled in your community. These plastics should never be thrown away with the rest of the trash. Most communities collect and recycle plastics with codes that look like this:

More to Explore

Lakes and Ponds • Metal • Plastic • Rivers and Streams • Trees

Trees

Trees are very tall plants with thick stems called trunks. Branches grow from the trunk of a tree, and leaves grow on the branches. The trunk and branches of trees are covered with bark. Trees give us shade and help cool the Earth. We also get many products from trees, such as fruits, nuts, and wood.

A tree's trunk and branches are covered with a layer of bark. Bark protects the tree. Bark can be rough or smooth. It can be thick or thin.

THE PARTS OF A TREE

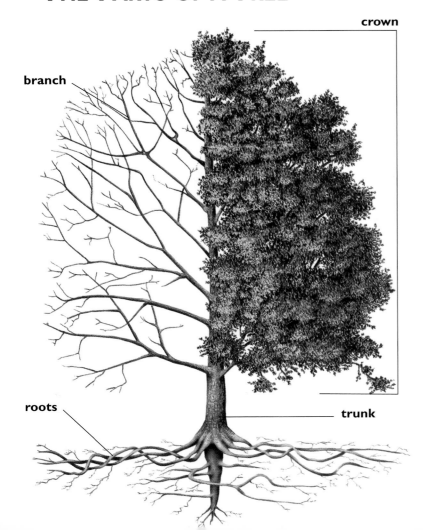

crown

branch

roots

trunk

TREE LEAVES

All trees have leaves, but the leaves do not look the same.

Deciduous (di-SI-joo-wuhs) trees have broad, flat leaves. The leaves turn colors and drop from the tree in the fall. New leaves grow in the spring.

Most evergreen trees have pointed leaves called *needles*. Needles do not drop from the tree during the fall. The tree looks the same all year.

More to Explore

Earth • Forests • Plants • The Seasons

149

U. S. Presidents

The leader of the United States of America is called the President. The President is chosen by the people of the United States every four years. The President is a very important person. He or she helps run the country and makes sure that everything is going well. The President is the most powerful person in the U.S. government.

It's a Fact!
The Fourth of July is an important day in the United States. It is the day the country celebrates its independence. Three Presidents—John Adams, Thomas Jefferson, and James Monroe—have died on the Fourth of July.

The President of the United States lives and works at the White House in the city of Washington, D.C.

Every four years, the people of the United States *vote,* or choose, who will become President. People 18 and older fill out a form to say who they want to be President. The person who gets the most votes becomes the next President.

Mount Rushmore in South Dakota has the faces of Presidents George Washington, Thomas Jefferson, Teddy Roosevelt, and Abraham Lincoln.

More to Explore

Democracy

Water

Water is one of the most important things on Earth. Every living thing must have water to survive. We need water to drink, to grow our food, and to wash things. Water is even used to make electricity.

Do you think water is stronger than rock? It takes thousands of years, but water is able to wear away rocks. This is called *erosion*. This is how canyons are made.

HOW WE GET WATER

When you want water, you just turn on a tap. But how does the water get there?

1. Water is collected in lakes or reservoirs.

2. The water is purified to take out dirt and things that could make you sick.

3. Clean water travels through pipes under the ground to homes and businesses.

4. Pipes carry the water inside buildings for us to use.

5. Waste water flows though pipes into sewers.

6. The waste water is treated so it can be used again.

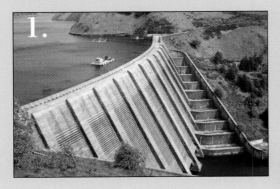

THE FORMS OF WATER

When you think about water, you probably think about it as a liquid. But water can also be a solid or a gas.

liquid

solid

gas

It's a Fact!
Did you know that there is water in your skin, your blood, the air in your lungs, and your muscles? In fact, most of your body is made of water.

We get energy from water. Falling or running water can be used to spin the blades of huge machines called *turbines.* As the turbines spin, they make electricity. The electricity travels through wires to where it is needed.

There is more water on the Earth than anything else. Water is everywhere. It's in oceans and lakes and rivers. It's even in little puddles!

Most of the water at the North and South Pole is frozen into ice. Sometimes a huge chunk of ice breaks off and falls into the ocean. The chunk of ice floats in the water, with just a small part of it showing. It is called an *iceberg*.

WASTING WATER

We cannot live without water. So it is important to take care of our water and not to waste it. It is also important to keep our water clean. Here are some things you can do.

• Turn the water off while you brush your teeth.

• Be sure faucets are off completely so they don't drip.

• Throw trash where it belongs so it can't get into the water.

• Take a shower instead of a bath.

• Be careful what you put down the drain. Things like oil and paint are bad for the Earth's water.

It's a Fact!

• Life on Earth started in the water. The first living things were plants that grew in the oceans. The first animals lived in the ocean, too. Millions of years passed before animals started to live on land.

• We get a lot of our food from the water. We eat fish and other water animals. Some people also eat water plants, such as seaweed.

More to Explore

Electricity • Lakes and Ponds • Ocean • Rivers and Streams • Rocks • Weather

Weather

Earth is surrounded by a warm, thick layer of air called the atmosphere. Weather is what happens in the atmosphere. Heat, cold, and wind are all parts of weather. So are rain, snow, sleet, and hail. Different parts of the world have different kinds of weather. The weather changes all the time.

Words to Know
expand: *get larger*

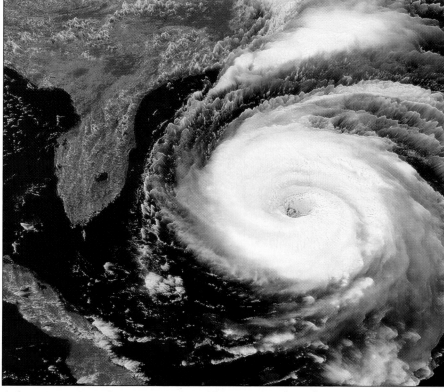

A hurricane is a huge rainstorm that starts over the ocean. Hurricane clouds pick up lots of water from the ocean. The water falls back to Earth as heavy rain. Hurricanes have strong winds, too. The wind can make waves that flood land near the ocean. The heavy rain can also cause floods farther away from the ocean.

LIGHTNING

Have you ever seen a spark when you walked across a rug and touched a doorknob? Your feet rubbing against the rug made electricity. When you touched the doorknob, the electricity moved from your body to the knob. The same kind of thing happens inside clouds to make lightning. Dust and drops of water move around and bump into each other. Electricity builds up until it moves to another cloud or to the ground. When it moves, it makes a big spark. That is lightning.

Thunder and lightning go together. Lightning heats up the air around it. The hot air moves so quickly that it makes a loud noise. That noise is thunder. So if you hear thunder, go inside. It means lightning is on the way!

HOW WATER MAKES WEATHER

Earth's atmosphere is full of water. Without this water, there would be no weather. As water moves and changes, it makes the weather. The way water moves is called the *water cycle.*

Step 1. The sun makes water *evaporate,* or turn into invisible water vapor.

Step 2. Water vapor cools off as it rises. It *condenses,* or turns into drops of water. Thousands of drops join together to form a cloud.

Step 3. Water falls from clouds back to Earth as rain, snow, hail, or sleet. This is called *precipitation.*

Step 4. Water that falls back to Earth flows into rivers, lakes, and the ocean. Some water goes underground, where it collects in pools.

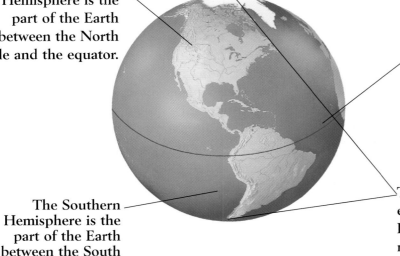

The Northern Hemisphere is the part of the Earth between the North Pole and the equator.

The equator is an imaginary line around the middle of the Earth. The area around it gets a lot of sunlight all year long. It is always warm.

The Southern Hemisphere is the part of the Earth between the South Pole and the equator.

The poles are at the ends of the Earth. Less light and heat reach these parts of the Earth. It is always cold at the poles.

Clouds are made up of thousands of tiny drops of water. The drops come together to form different kinds of clouds. Many kinds of clouds bring rainy weather. But there are clouds in the sky on sunny days, too.

A tornado is a huge windstorm. Tornadoes only form during thunderstorms. Sometimes part of a storm cloud starts to swirl. It forms a funnel shape that reaches down from the sky. The winds in the funnel move in circles and go hundreds of miles an hour. When a tornado touches the ground, it causes a lot of damage.

It's a Fact!
• There are many different colors of light. Sunlight looks blue when it shines through the air. That is why the sky looks blue to us.
• A hurricane can be 500 miles wide. Tornadoes are smaller. The part of a tornado that touches the ground is usually less than a mile wide.
• Fog is like a cloud that is on the ground. Sometimes you can actually see the drops of water in fog.

A thermometer measures the temperature of the air. Many thermometers have liquid inside a glass tube. When the air is warm, it makes the liquid expand and take up more space. The liquid moves up in the tube. When the air is cool, the liquid takes up less space. It moves down in the tube.

WHEN RAIN FREEZES

Snow is frozen rain. When it is very cold, raindrops inside the clouds freeze. They turn into snowflakes and fall to Earth. Snowflakes are made of ice crystals. Different-shaped crystals join together to make each snowflake. With so many shapes to put together, every snowflake looks different.

Hail is frozen rain, too. A frozen raindrop is called a *hailstone.* Hailstones are larger than snowflakes, and they melt more slowly. That is why hailstones can fall in the summer when the air is warm.

Wind is moving air. When sunlight warms the air that is close to Earth, the air rises. Colder air sinks to the ground and takes the warmer air's place. The rising and falling movements of the air create wind.

More to Explore

Colors • Earth • Electricity • Light • The Seasons • Water

Wetlands

Wetlands are places where the land is always covered with shallow water. They are found all around the world. Most wetlands are called swamps, marshes, or bogs. Many plants and animals live in wetlands.

Words to Know
shallow: *not deep*

Swamps are always wet, but the water level can change. If there is a lot of rain, the water gets deeper. If the water in a swamp stays deep enough to cover the tree roots, the trees can die.

THE DIFFERENT WETLANDS

Marshes, swamps, and bogs are different. Grassy plants and bushes grow in a marsh, but trees do not. A swamp has bushes and trees. A bog is formed when dead plants pile up and make a thick, spongy layer. A bog is a lot like a wet mattress!

The water in a bog doesn't move very much. It just sits in one place. Some types of plants love growing in this still water.

Marshes can have freshwater or saltwater. Freshwater marshes are found near the edges of lakes, ponds, and rivers. Saltwater marshes are usually near the ocean. Salty ocean water mixes with freshwater from ponds, lakes, and rivers near the shore.

More to Explore

Lakes and Ponds • Ocean • Plants • Rivers and Streams • Water

Index